HOUSE OF COMMONS LIBRARY

LOCATION	R Etiquette
AUTHOR	Anderson
Acc DATE	29 MAY 1996

TO BE
DISPOSED
BY
AUTHORITY

GENTILITY RECALLED

GENTILITY RECALLED

Mere Manners and the Making of Social Order

Edited by
DIGBY ANDERSON

Published by The Social Affairs Unit
and The Acton Institute For The Study Of Religion And Liberty

©The Social Affairs Unit 1996
All Rights Reserved

British Library Cataloguing in Publication Data
A catalogue record of this book is available from
the British Library

ISBN 0 907631 66 5

IN MEMORY OF FRANK SANDERSON
FOUNDER TRUSTEE AND LONG-TERM BENEFACTOR
OF THE SOCIAL AFFAIRS UNIT
AND A GENTLEMAN OF PERFECT MANNERS

We gratefully acknowledge the support of the
Lynde and Harry Bradley Foundation
towards the work that made this book possible

Social Affairs Unit publications represent the views of their individual authors, not those of the Unit, its Director, Trustees or Advisers

Book production and typesetting by Crowley Esmonde Ltd
Printed and bound in Great Britain by St Edmundsbury Press Ltd

Contents

The Authors

Professor Michael D Aeschliman taught English at Columbia and the University of Virginia for ten years and is now Director of the Erasmus Institute, Lausanne, Switzerland. He is author of *The Restitution of Man: C S Lewis and the case against scientism* and edited a new paperback edition of Malcolm Muggeridge's 1934 novel *Winter in Moscow*. He has written widely for journals on both sides of the Atlantic. His selection of essays by John Henry Newman will be published shortly.

Dr Digby Anderson is founder Director of the Social Affairs Unit and editor of the Unit's series *The Moral Dimension of Social Policy*. He was contributing editor of *The Loss of Virtue: moral confusion and social disorder in Britain and America* and of *This Will Hurt: the restoration of virtue and civic order* which were both published as National Review books. He is a regular contributor to journals and newspapers.

Dr Bruce Charlton MD is a lecturer in public health medicine at the University of Newcastle upon Tyne. He has previously worked as a psychiatrist, medical scientist and a lecturer in human anatomy. Publications on health policy include articles in the *British Medical Journal*, *The Lancet* and *The Times*, and contributions to *Preventionitis* (SAU, 1994) and *The Sociology of Health Promotion* (Routledge, 1995).

Professor H Tristram Engelhardt Jr is Professor in the Department of Medicine, Baylor College of Medicine, Houston and in the Department of Philosophy, Rice University, and Member of the Center for Medical Ethics and Health Policy. He is editor of *The Journal of Medicine and Philosophy* and co-editor of *Christian Bioethics*. A thoroughly revised version of his book, *The Foundations of Bioethics*, will be appearing in a second edition through Oxford University Press.

Dr Robert Grant is Reader in English Literature at the University of Glasgow and former Fellow of Trinity Hall, Cambridge. He is the author of *Oakeshott* (Claridge Press, 1990) and of many articles and reviews in *Inquiry*, *Philosophical Quarterly*, *Shakespeare Studies*, *The Times Literary Supplement* and elsewhere. He has lectured widely in the United States and Eastern Europe.

Dr Simon Green is a Fellow of All Souls' College, Oxford, and Lecturer in Modern History in the University of Leeds. He is the author of *Religion in the Age of Decline: organization and experience in the West Riding of Yorkshire, c 1870-1920* and Editor (with R C Whiting) of *The Boundaries of State in Modern Britain*. He has also written numerous articles on various aspects of nineteenth and twentieth century British history, public policy and political philosophy.

Dr Athena S Leoussi studied at the University of Grenoble, the Courtauld Institute of Art and the London School of Economics. She is Lecturer in Sociology at the University of Reading, Chair of the Association for the Study of Ethnicity and Nationalism (ASEN) which is based at LSE, and editor of the journal *Nations and Nationalism*. She has contributed articles to the *Dictionary of Art* (Macmillan, 1996) and her books, *The Ionides Circle and Art* and *Nationalism and Classicism in Nineteenth Century England and France*, will be published shortly.

Professor George Martin is Chairman of the English Department at Wofford College, Spartanburg, South Carolina, having previously taught at the University of Georgia. His main academic interest is in sixteenth and seventeenth century English literature and he has published articles on Shakespeare and Milton and is currently writing a book on the latter's conception of evil in *Paradise Lost*.

Caroline Moore was the first woman Fellow of Peterhouse, Cambridge and Director of Studies in English, from 1985 to 1990. She left to give birth to twins, and is now a full-time mother and part-time book reviewer for the *Sunday Telegraph*, *The Spectator* and *The Times*.

Professor Anthony O'Hear is Professor of Philosophy at the University of Bradford and Honorary Director of the Royal Institute of Philosophy. He is author of many books and articles on philosophy, and a frequent contributor to the national press. He is a member of the School Curriculum and Assessment Authority, and of the Teacher Training Agency.

Professor John Shelton Reed is William Rand Kenan Jr Professor of Sociology, Director of the Institute for Research in Social Science, and Chairman of the Center for the Study of the American South at the University of North Carolina. The most recent of his dozen books is *1001 Things Everyone Should Know about the South* (with Dale Volberg Reed). He writes regularly for *Chronicles: A Magazine of American Culture.*

Rachel Trickett was Principal of St Hugh's College, Oxford from 1973 until her retirement in 1991; she is now an Honorary Fellow of the College. She is author of *The Honest Muse*, a study in Augustan verse, and of several novels.

Foreword

Bryan Wilson*

* Bryan Wilson FBA is Emeritus Fellow of All Souls and Reader Emeritus in Sociology in the University of Oxford, where he taught for over 30 years.

Manners: old-fashioned but still in demand

'Manners'! The word itself has come to have an old-fashioned ring. One is reminded of the anxious exhortation of pre-war mothers dispatching children to the care of relatives or neighbours, '...and mind your manners!', or of the catch phrase (wherever did it come from — the Victorian music hall perhaps?) 'Manners, girls! Boys have none'. Manners, and the idea of manners, were in those days a conscious concern, and as these two everyday quotations indicate, not solely for the middle classes, but also for the common people. What had once been the subject of instruction for the gentry, had become part of a proud inheritance of ordinary folk, confirming their claim to be part of the 'respectable working class', and investing them with a keenly-felt sense of dignity and decorum.

Times have changed: on the threshold of the millennium, the very notion of manners appears to many people to be antiquated if not obsolete, an overly precious concern for the genteel, and for others, albeit perhaps a small yet influential minority, to be evidence of a conspiracy of upper classes to ensure deference and orderly behaviour from the masses. Yet, even today, there remains widespread recognition that society is as much in need of the values implicit in manners as ever it was. People deprecate the break-down of common decency in public places, complain about the lack of courtesy in shops, condemn as 'uncivilized' behaviour incidental to contemporary wars — in Bosnia or Rwanda. Our demand for decency, courtesy, and civilized comportment is a demand for the maintenance of manners and their transmission from generation to generation. It is a demand for predictability of conduct, restraint on passions, and the maintenance of goodwill in normal social intercourse.

Spitting and guffawing: the refinement of 'natural' behaviour
The process of civilization has been a process of the refinement of behaviour (refinement — another term disparaged in our own times!). Teaching people how, when, and where to discharge bodily functions, and — more important since culture is primarily a set of interdictions — how, when, and where not to do so (to spit, to blow one's nose, to urinate) has played an essential role in the creation of modern civilization. All of these and many other aspects of bodily control, which the naive have supposed to be purely 'natural' reactions to stimuli, are responses learned under the direction of manners. Even involuntary behaviour, coughing, sneezing, and laughing, is subject to internal discipline — society demands that it should be. To drive home the power of social training ie, manners, a distinguished psychologist once observed that 'the laugh that is normal in a mill-girl would be diagnostic of mania in a nun'. Both mill-girl and nun had learned, by imitation and habit in the culture and according to the manners of the communities to which they respectively belonged, how (and when and where) to laugh. If such semi-instinctive elements of behaviour have been moulded by manners, how much more so has this been the case with the more fully conscious aspects of comportment. The civilizing process, the gentling of the people, became, over the course of centuries, an increasingly institutionalized concern in western societies, forming a vital part of public education as well as of the socialization of children in the family.

Manners a victim of a more general de-moralization
Why, then, by the latter part of the twentieth century, have the cultivation of refinement and the inculcation of manners not only fallen into so much neglect, but become the objects of so much open ridicule and contempt? No doubt the causes are complex, but the major element has been the steady *de*-moralization of society in the modern era. Societies were once held together as integrated and coherent systems by a widely shared value consensus, a common *mentalité*, a pervasive moral consciousness. Men identified with the community in which they lived, regarding its folkways and mores as god-given and *right*. People appraised the community itself, its objective possessions, and the comportment of its members in common moral terms. Their decisions and choices were governed not by rational or

technical criteria, but by traditional conceptions of custom and virtue. Older people were perceived as wiser because they had a longer experience of the moral ethos. Society was a moralized domain, and all aspects of comportment were not matters of indifference, but were subject to moral judgement.

Collective moral judgements informed people how to comport themselves, not only in their active behaviour, but even in such apparently minor matters as the way in which they dressed, the speech patterns which they employed, the way they walked. Such were the concerns that Hobbes called 'small morals'. To take an example: there was appropriate dress and inappropriate dress (I remember as recently as four decades ago — and I do not think that I was an exceptionally 'moralized' individual — being shocked on first seeing people in downtown New York dressed as if they were on holiday: now many people in Britain appear to be on holiday, or *en route* for a fancy dress — or undress — ball, any or all of the time). Nor was this merely an upper or middle class phenomenon: working people too had appropriate dress — working clothes and Sunday clothes. The differences were to be respected, since clothes themselves deserved respect and needed to be cared for. In contrast, modern youth, in expendable jeans, the more esteemed if torn and dirty, squats lightly on any filthy pavement, and, in punk or grunge style, reinforces the message that anything goes: respect for things becomes as alien as respect for persons.

Manners decline as moral judgement gives way to causal explanation

The *de*-moralization of society has been a many-sided process and has proceeded from many causes. One has been the shift of the touchstone of behavioural rectitude from moral judgement to causal explanation, manifested in the growth of a therapeutic orientation, which, in rejecting the categories of blame and virtue, increasingly de-moralizes conduct. There has been a diminution of culpability, and a corresponding increase in excusability: 'it's not his fault — it's the system' or 'he's not wicked, he's sick', and a willingness to pass off both criminality and a lack of manners under the rubric of 'self-expression' or the individual's endeavour to 'tell us something'. Since the expectation of mannerly behaviour demands only the lightest form of restraint on the individual, empowered by the mildest of sanctions (public ridicule or disapprobation) it is manners that have experienced the most direct onslaught of *de*-moralization.

As values have been relativized, so morals and manners have been eviscerated. When society enjoyed one more or less coherent system of values and an authoritative agency to communicate them and superintend their transmission from one generation to the next, those values could be embodied as the prescriptive manners of everyday behaviour. But as value consensus was challenged, old normative certainties yielded to alternative formulae, to the ever-present undercurrent urges of primitive passions, of uncaring, impulse-ridden self-expression, and of self-interest before social obligation. Social diversification, mass immigration, and even, most recently, the misplaced transfer to the substantive social order itself of the demand for ethical neutrality in the social sciences, have all contributed to the relativization of values and the contingent circumstance of moral uncertainty and the subversion of normative order as represented by mannerly comportment. This relativity was earliest encountered in America, and one sees why Jefferson, as a founder of the first self-consciously 'man-made' society, engaged in the vain attempt to devise for the new country a code of manners. But mannerly behaviour cannot be enforced by conscious and deliberate planning: manners must grow spontaneously in propitious social locales, and *then* be cultivated.

Technical, contractual competence replaces goodwill and respect

The operation of the social system no longer relies on widespread moral consensus. Technological knowledge has replaced dependence on moral and mannerly dispositions: the demand for predictability in social life has come to rely on more precise and calculated procedures of technically-specified patterns of interaction. The individual increasingly becomes a role-player, his responses contractually specified, and his performances impersonally defined and executed. His personal virtue becomes irrelevant to his performance in his work-role, which is judged entirely by technical criteria. Since the work-order influences all other areas in which people interact, so its style infects all aspects of everyday life. Reliance on technical competence reduces dependence on personal goodwill, inherent grace, gestures of respect, and hence the self-esteem that looks for confirmation in the esteem of others.

Not the least significant aspect of technological change is the premium which it puts on youth. The young learn new techniques, and their technical skill renders obsolete the skills and expertise of earlier decades. In consequence, older workers, once prized as 'experienced hands', increasingly find that long experience, instead of enhancing the esteem in which they are held, simply renders them 'has-beens'. Such considerations should not, one might suppose, influence the moral sphere. Clearly, moral wisdom, unlike technical knowledge, is not subject to innovative adjustments: it is slowly acquired and subject to little if any supersession. Yet such is the prestige of technology, that the older generation, the 'has-beens' of the work sphere (and in an age of communications revolution, of other spheres, too — markedly in leisure and recreation) are also easily regarded as has-beens in the moral domain. Their manners and their moral sense mark them out as yesterday's men: what relevance can their conscious regard for respectful social comportment have for the realities of this radically changed world?

Manners assailed by leftists and libertarians

The decline of manners has occurred not solely as a spontaneous and unconscious reaction to the technological innovation of recent decades: it has been furthered by a steady and sustained assault from various quarters. Ideologically, the political supporters of the far left have indicted manners as a device by which the middle classes served the ruling classes by systematic indoctrination to render tractable the poor. Libertarian commentators and trendy liberal intellectuals have ridiculed the received norms of social intercourse, cutting through convention in the name of freedom. The upsurge of violence among students in the backwash of the hippy movement of the mid and late 1960s may not have had manners as its primary target, but manners were certainly one of the intended victims of the assault. That revolution failed in its immediate, overt objectives, but the process of attrition which has relentlessly followed has seen the debasement of social order and the marked deterioration of the standards of everyday civil behaviour fully in conformity with the political ideals which the revolution failed to achieve. The counter-culture with its permissive, libertarian lifestyle penetrated the core of British society, and made especially powerful inroads into the newly powerful institutions through which social values were disseminated — the entertainment industry, advertising, and the media. One need look no further than the recurrent controversy concerning the language used in these so-called industries. Concern not to give offence, once a guiding maxim taken over from the manners of private individuals, has been replaced by the desire to shock, to dare, and to be noticed. Primitive impulses are played upon and stimulated, and the feast of misrule, once the regulated and very occasional safety-valve for an ordered society, becomes the veritable (dis)order of the day. A modern play, novel, comedy sketch, or broadcast makes almost mandatory use of what was once 'bad language'. To roll back the frontiers of civic politeness becomes almost a manifesto for these virtually uncontrolled agencies of communication. To their mission they bring technological sophistication of a kind quite unequalled by the relative amateurism of those ancient communicators whose concern was the diffusion of public morals and manners — the family, the churches, the schools, and perhaps above all the Sunday schools — once attended by some half of the child population, and now in sad decline. Should it be wondered that manners deteriorate, given the *de*-moralizing influences that are assiduously at work?

From a producer to a consumer society: restraint replaced by hedonism

Alongside the process of technological change which undermined the sort of society which depended for its cohesion on shared moral consciousness has been another change which has affected manners — the shift from a producer to a consumer society. In the producer societies of the past, in which there was scarcity of resources, the prevailing conditions demanded of most people that they work, save, put by what little they could for the future, and hence postpone present gratification. Scarcity demanded self-restraint and self-denial, which was made less harrowing by an ascetic ethic, a morality of forbearance, and the promise that virtue was its own reward for the righteous. Improved techniques of production gradually mitigated scarcity, led to surplus production, and created an entirely new economic emphasis. Steadily, the balance shifted, from the stimulus to produce and the ascetic ethic that supported it to a stimulus to consume. People were urged to buy, to use, even to waste resources.

The ethic changed: hedonism replaced asceticism. New agencies disseminating these new values — the agencies of advertising and entertainment — dislodged the old agencies of value-dissemination, the churches. Self-restraint was out, self-indulgence was in. As advertising campaigns told people to relax, to claim their deserts, to indulge themselves as much as they could, and popular songs proclaimed 'Enjoy yourself, enjoy yourself, it's later than you think', so a new ethos was brought into being and systematically reinforced.

Such a course of change could not but affect manners. The former economic and ethical underpinning of mannerly behaviour was eroded. These changes, together with new work patterns; commuting; the breakdown of local communities; the increased dependence on people as role-players rather than as total persons; the growth of bureaucracy; the increased size of institutions (companies, schools, recreational and entertainment facilities, and the media) — have all added to the impersonality of social contexts. And so have rendered apparently less important personal virtue and the need to behave towards known others in ways that would not give offence. Road rage; noisy neighbours; local vandalism; street aggression; and other manifestations of deliberate offensiveness, the result of a lack of manners, occur because other people are no longer seen to deserve treatment as dignified equals.

Any hope for a return to manners?

If so much has been lost, what hope is there for the preservation of those patterns of conduct which, in inducing self-restraint and self-control, defuse conflict and facilitate peace and goodwill in society? Certainly, we cannot legislate to command mannerliness: Burke saw that manners did not depend on laws, rather the opposite, since laws touched people's lives only intermittently and unevenly. Nor can we follow Jefferson in trying to devise a conscious code of manners for a new type of society. The present-day parallel version of manners for a 'brave new world', promulgated supposedly to civilize modern man, Political Correctness, is a transparently artificial, alien, rigid, and mechanical code that lacks the essential mainsprings of common sense, common consent, and common conscience. Apart from its fascist disposition to impose standards, it manifests the same symptomatic self-contradiction as the demand of 1960s students in Berkeley that there should be set up a 'committee to establish community'.

Perhaps our best hope is to turn to the example of those agencies which have sustained their own ethic, which have socialized their intake of successive generations, which have established norms of self-discipline, and which have provided models of civilized comportment, goodwill, social service, and high levels of personal self-sacrifice for the common good. I refer of course to the professions, and take my cue from Emile Durkheim, who saw in them the best prospect of reprieve from the predatory values of rampant commercialism. It is a slender life-line in a period when government, endorsing current economic trends, has systematically sought to undermine one profession after another, turning everyone, from patients and passengers, litigants and pupils, into mere customers, and subjecting professional services, henceforth called 'products', to inappropriate 'market' models. The erosion of the professional ethic, were recent policies to be sustained and continued, would be a further blow to mannerly social values and civility in relationships. If gentility is to be restored, perhaps our first step should be to seek to preserve and reinforce those few remaining agencies in which civic goodwill and an independent service ethic still survives.

INTRODUCTION AND SUMMARY

The Little Things that Matter

Trivia and the Maintenance of Social Order

Digby Anderson

What is offensive is not necessarily an offence

It is a warm, peaceful summer's evening. After dinner, a middle-class couple are drinking coffee and talking in their drawing room with two dinner guests. The house is in a respectable area. The drawing room overlooks a small front garden largely filled with roses. Suddenly there is the noise of raucous laughter from the garden. A band of young people have pushed their way from the street, through the gate and are busy relieving themselves all over the garden, one girl hooting with crude amusement as she squats like some animal among the bushes. In the same garden, a while before, the householder had found used condoms hung on the railings.

In a similarly respectable area during the daytime, a 70 year-old woman is driving her car. She is driving a little slowly and hesitantly because she is looking for a particular house and the numbers on the doors are difficult to see. A 40 year-old man following her drives as close as he can to the back of her car, suddenly sounds his horn, swerves and roars past, waving his fist and yelling that people of her age should either drive properly or get off the road altogether.

Such incidents have several important features. The most important is that while their victims find them deeply shocking, criminologists classify them as trivial. Though the behaviour is deeply offensive, it is not a 'serious offence', perhaps not an 'offence' at all. In Britain, the criminologists and bureaucrats at the Home Office have long contended that there is not as much crime as many ordinary people suppose. Indeed, ordinary people's misconceptions about crime levels are held by some criminologists to be as serious a problem, even a more serious problem than crime itself. It is not so much the crimes of criminals, but the public's 'fear of crime' which is the problem. Not only, say such criminologists, is there not as much crime as the hysterical public believes, but much of the crime that is committed is not serious. It is just minor thefts, burglary, that sort of thing, not physical violence.

Worries about 'law and order' essentially worries about 'order'

In fact, the criminologists are partly correct in their account, though wholly wrong in their judgement. Many of the acts that upset decent people are not punishable by long jail sentences. They are not serious offences, some not offenses at all. However, just because they are legally trivial, it does not mean that they are not extremely upsetting and serious for those obliged to suffer them. And here we come to the point: that the huge number of trivial offences and the even greater number of not illegal anti-social incidents that characterize modern society, may, in fact, worry ordinary people *more* than the fewer 'serious' offenses. When ordinary people express concern about 'law and order', what concerns them may be the hundreds of little incidents rather than the few serious ones. People in general are more concerned about order or the lack of it than they are about law-abiding behaviour or the lack of it. Yet when academics and politicians use the phrase 'law and order' they usually restrict their interest to law. Of course, the rallying moments for popular indignation will be celebrated criminal cases such as the battering of a child or the raping of an 80 year-old lady. But what fuels the indignation is the squatting in the roses or the even less serious impatience of the overtaking driver.

As so often, ordinary people's analysis of social problems may be more refined than that of experts. It is experts who crudely categorize problems into 'big' and 'small'. Ordinary people know, from experience, that large numbers of small problems may be worse than occasional big ones. To move away from the criminal problems altogether, it is certainly the case that large numbers of big problems, say the huge explosion of single-parent families, cause damage to the children concerned, hardship to the remaining parent, and impose enormous costs on two-parent taxpayers struggling to maintain their families. But it is also the case that much larger numbers of parents and especially elderly parents are hurt, every day in countless, unrecorded instances of trivial neglect and rudeness by their children. Young parents are taken for granted. Difficult elderly parents are not visited. And the graves of dead parents are left to grow over with weeds.

The attack on manners

The vast amount of suffering caused by 'small' and 'trivial' incidents is, in part, the domain of manners. Some manners are the outward manifestation of internal morals. Even when they are not, when they are simply mechanical, it may be that the lack of 'trivial' manners causes more social damage and unhappiness than the lack of heroic morals. This is difficult to accept. Long before the 1960s, the triviality of manners had been derided by those who prided themselves on thinking big. There was only one term of abuse stronger than 'bourgeois' and that was 'petit-bourgeois' with its connotations, in English use, of the trite and unimaginative. The decadent 1890s, Freud (or rather his disciples), Bloomsbury, the Marxists, and the flowering of them all in the 1960s, could at least agree on this: their contempt for little men and their mindless daily habits, their manners. Some of them did not have overmuch time for morals either, but at least morals were about 'big' things. In the 1960s, manners were condemned for being artificial as opposed to natural, restrictive as opposed to liberating, habitual as opposed to thoughtful or 'critical', mechanical as opposed to existentially committed, hierarchical as opposed to open or equal, hypocritical as opposed to genuine or straightforward, traditional as opposed to progressive.

There were counter voices. Perhaps surprisingly, one of the strongest came from within social science and reached a peak in those same 1960s. Anthropologists, in particular, brought massive evidence of the role of the daily, repeated, tiny acts of culture in maintaining social order. Sociologists started to study much 'smaller' fragments of social interaction, conversations, dress, body language, in order to show how order was achieved from second to second. It did not last. Or rather it had little impact on the wider understanding of society. The analysts of ritual, gesture and conversation were dismissed as irrelevant: irrelevant to the major themes of class struggle, anti-racism and the new revolution against bourgeois cultural hegemony. In an age when not to be political was to be politically reactionary, these 'micro' social scientists were not joining the barricades. What had body language to do with liberating the poor?

Perhaps quite a lot. That is what we can now see. A society which takes its manners seriously may not change the 'big' aspects of any one group of people: it may not make the poor rich. But it does make society easier and better for everyone. And if that sounds too strong, consider the opposite. A society which does not value the quality of the millions of daily acts that happen between its members, but only the grand themes of policies and politics, will leave all its members worse off in their daily lives.

Manners were not examined and argued against in the 1960s. There was no sustained attempt to improve manners by weeding out the silly or outdated and retaining the sensible. They were dismissed as manners because they were manners. Life was to be individual and experimental, constructed with the dawn of each new day to fit the newly pondered needs of authentic self-expression. The onslaught did not, of course, mean that manners obediently disappeared. If they are indeed essential for orderly society, then their disappearance would mean not just the coarseness of current Britain and America, but chaos. We still stick by rules of common language and gesture. How could we do otherwise and survive as a society?

Indeed, one could argue that most manners have survived. But not all, and the ones which have do not exert the same force. With manners, small shifts can have enormous consequences. This is largely because manners are to do with predictability. Citizens who can count on manners can feel secure and at ease. Once the garden has been invaded, the driver insulted several times, once familiarly safe territory has been violated, once safe times to go here or there, to do this or that with predictable consequences, have been cast into doubt or thrown into confusion, then citizens become apprehensive, circumspect, nervous or afraid. They have to think about making journeys, saying things, doing things they never thought about before.

The criminologists are correct in that most people do not suffer grievous assault or rape. But the truth is that one does not have to reach for the extremity of rape to demonstrate the roughness on the streets, or to total family collapse to show the day to day rudeness of young to older people. Citizens who have never been raped or robbed are still treated daily to countless small incidents which make them fearful. The crisis in order is a crisis in manners. Respectable, middle-class people going about their normal routines in the street, the train station, the shop or the park, increasingly feel that these are not *their* streets, stations and parks, but occupied territory. Or just territory that *may* be hostile, where you have to look around, hold your bag, or be out of by dusk.

Small inconveniences are, because frequent, the largest aspect of civic breakdown

So, the actual incidence of crime is not the sole, nor perhaps even the principal element of the sense of collapse of civic order which many feel. The sense of intimidation and mistrust which may be felt when encountering a group of young men in the street may not be justified by any violent predisposition from that group of individuals, but it is no less real for that. Despite the mammoth public expenditure on local government, streets strewn with litter help to foster the impression that there is a physical decay in our towns and cities.

The fear of an elderly and frail person living alone that neighbours cannot be relied upon to summon help in the event of an accident is all too understandable at a time when many inhabitants of cities can hardly name another individual in their neighbourhood. And the breakdown of relationships is clearly indicated by the spectacle of supposedly sophisticated societies which require legal agreements between couples during progressive stages of courtship, allow children to 'divorce' their parents, and require cumbersome legislation to divide in public places those who smoke from those who do not.

It is true that people do worry about the mega-issues which top the electoral tactics charts such as unemployment and taxes. But what draws letters to the popular press and causes indignation in countless hairdressers and pubs are tales of lack of consideration, petty selfishness, forgetfulness of others, and boorishness. Ordinary people are acutely conscious of the distress caused by being jostled in crowded streets with no word of apology or the threatening nature of the deliberately war-like clothing of some young men. They are affronted by the lack of courtesy which accompanies many simple and everyday transactions. Buying a loaf of bread, boarding a bus or an appointment with their own doctor has become a trial.

The loss of manners and the loss of ease and predictions

These events may, in themselves, seem trivial matters. But the abandonment of basic mannerly behaviour is, suggest the authors of this book, both an indication of and possible cause of the factors which conspire to create the destruction of shared civic values. At the least, the abandonment of manners has made life less comfortable, less predictable. This small thing is no small thing. Without the expectation of fairly predictable responses when dealing with fellow-citizens, incomprehension, inarticulacy and offence quickly characterize discourse. Businessmen (who might carefully study the customs of their counterparts in foreign countries) without basic skills of courtesy may find that they cannot communicate with those with whom they wish to do business at home. Banks and shops find that their customers are reluctant to deal with incompetent and impertinent staff; people of different generations find that they cannot talk together easily.

The rediscovery and habitual adoption of manners one solution to these large-scale problems

Manners, suggest the authors of the book, oil the wheels when these different groups interact. They provide a shared and understood pattern of behaviour in social intercourse, and allow, through a recognition of the differences which might otherwise separate individuals, spontaneous and productive exchanges. Part of the strength of manners is precisely the informality and flexibility which they allow when they are automatic, instinctive and ingrained. Simply, they make everything very much easier.

Prejudice can, or course, be an unpleasant and dangerous thing. But the 'useful' prejudices which manners instill allow a stability and spontaneity in discourse and encounters between people who may be from different or 'unequal' backgrounds or, indeed, competing interests. This easiness is precisely what is missing from the cumbersome codes of behaviour which have sprung up in an attempt to replace manners. Only when courteous behaviour is as ingrained as manners can be, when the process of opening doors, deferring to the infirm or elderly, remembering to say 'please' and 'thank you' is automatic, unthinking, is there the possibility of ease of this sort in encounters between people. The legalistic codes of political correctness and charters drawn up by civil servants and governments can never supply the same instinctive readiness. But the correctness codes are a useful piece of evidence in the manners debate. What they do is to admit that some regulation of, eg, relationships between men and women is needed. Several of the targets of PC codes are activities in which one person's pleasure may be another's pain. Two are sex-relations and smoking. The codes give guidance on how to behave. So did manners. Mannerly societies recognize that their members will seek pleasure and that in so doing they may hurt others. They also realize that general injunctions not to hurt others are insufficient. So, in such societies manners are evolved which govern courting habits or the relations between smokers and non-smokers. Another example is with the consumption of alcohol. Essentially manners are ways of making potentially harmful pleasures and even vices, harmless or less harmful. They do this not only by setting controls of time and place and sequence but by socializing young people into such behaviour. Sensible societies do not, for instance, forbid young people to drink alcohol until they are adults but socialize them into drinking from an early age. They also acquire social institutions for drinking, such as pubs, which themselves have their own codes which informally regulate drinking. The achievement of manners is to control behaviour without the use of law or government and through custom and informal community sanctions. In contrast with the evolving, sophisticated control by manners, control by political correctness committee is clumsy and, because it often involves explicit legalistic rules and monitoring, oppressive.

The need for modern society to learn again the extent and sophistication of manners

It has been argued that manners are almost the epitome of 'repression' and 'inauthenticity', two concepts which earned the scorn of progressive academics and politicians, especially in the 1960s. In the rush for 'self-expression', many of the manners which prevented unchecked gratification and allowed easy social relations were abandoned. Manners were also spurned as relics of an outmoded class system, rather than seen as the means by which people of different backgrounds could meet within a code of behaviour based on shared values.

The behaviour of and between gentlemen and ladies was an early target of radical feminists, those who were keen to remove not only inequality, but all realistic distinctions between the sexes. Some of these distinctions were indeed small. But the assault on the manners of the sexes has gone far beyond castigating what was once thought solicitous — offering a bus seat to a lady — as patronizing. Crusading against patriarchy and Eurocentrism and in the name of feminism and multi-culturalism, progressives have effectively voted to annihilate the understanding of what it is to be a man or a woman, especially a gentleman or a lady in everyday life. The manners, the codes, the rules once covered everything. They gave men and women ways to behave, virtues and appearances to take on, ways of relating to each other, conduct for this, that and every occasion. That understanding was built up over years. It was a wisdom. It is now derided and in its place are put slogans, charters, and politically initiated directives on behaviour. Manners have always had to change in history. What is happening now is not gradual organic change but ideologically driven political correctness, much of it based on a poor understanding of past sex role manners. What is needed today is not a reinstatement of Victorian manners. That would be impossible. What is needed is an interest in manners, in what they were and could be, rather than their dismissal. That is the interest of this book: in reminding people of the vast beneficial role that manners played and might still play.

It is only when one starts to recall the various sophisticated aspects of manners, the essential tasks they perform, and the millions of tiny incidents that make up that performance, that one understands what a treasure-trove manners provide, and what an act of profligacy it is to attempt to dispense with them. This book makes no attempt to examine every one of the gems it offers. It takes a selection, such as the obvious differences between the sexes which are examined in chapters on the idea of a lady and of a gentleman. The etiquette of dress, important through almost all societies and times, is another clear example of the way in which others can be put at their ease, or offended, by what may seem a minor matter. Dr Simon Green examines the way in which sport can teach and develop manners, while other chapters look at upbringing in the family and home, and the examples set by behaviour between those of different generations. Even vices, which we cannot expect to banish completely, can be made tolerable by manners. These and other issues dealt with by the authors are not even the beginnings of a comprehensive list. But they give an indication of just how much may depend on seemingly tiny and unimportant matters.

The development of artificial self-control is essential to the manners of a gentleman

The ideal of the gentleman which developed from the middle of the nineteenth century is one where individuals are judged on behaviour rather than by rank or wealth. This change provided the opportunity for the courtly tradition, identified by both Caroline Moore in her historical analysis of the gentleman's role and in Rachel Trickett's survey of representative ideas of what constituted a lady, to move from the aristocracy to the emergent middle classes and beyond in the Victorian era. Caroline Moore notes that the notion of the gentleman is seen today as an artificial one, held in place by snobbery and hypocritical conventions which deceive only the gullible. Those who adhere to its ideals are dismissed as witless buffoons or hopelessly pompous characters divorced from the modern world. Conventions of artificial self-control, seen as self-repression by the Romantics, are even less popular with those who think self-control impossible because of 'the subconscious'.

But in fact the codes of the gentleman's behaviour are precisely what allow him the freedom to act naturally as an individual whilst taking a place in society. Tradition is not a narrow straitjacket. It is various, offers possibilities for behaviour within shared assumptions and it is what enables communities to exist and individuals to act within them, rather than merely at their behest. Being a gentleman has to do with mores rather than money, and shared ways of behaving do not entail uniform behaviour on any given occasion. The Victorian notion of the gentleman determined by behaviour rather than birth was a reaction to changes in class and previously fixed standards of judging character and behaviour. It was designed to liberate character from accident of birth or income. If a sense of self-respect was connected with a properly respectful appreciation of rank, it was not subordinate to it. The example of the gamekeeper in Kingsley's *Yeast* demonstrates the importance of behaviour, not wealth. 'Let the rich be as rich as they will. I, and those like me, covet not money, but manners.'

These spontaneous manners characteristic of the gentleman are an imitation of the ideal of Christian charity and, as with the liberty found in religious submission, only gentlemen possessed of Godly manners were truly capable of self-government.

The role of women has been falsified and undermined by radical feminism: rather than offering equality, it denies opportunity

Similarly, Rachel Trickett's chapter examines the way in which the idea of a lady has been associated with excessive refinement, at least since Chaucer's days. However, she points out the notion gave way to a more sophisticated and independent view of the proper attributes of womanliness. This is seen in the characters of Shakespeare's heroines, an example followed and developed by the novelists of the eighteenth and early nineteenth centuries.

By Jane Austen's time it was clear that a lady, like a gentleman could not be created by rank alone, and nineteenth century writers tended to confer the title on those women who demonstrated grace, warmth and loyalty, combined with moral intelligence, as their chief characteristics. Recent modern fiction, with its lack of interest in individual moral character (or in some cases, character *tout court*) ridicules this view. Yet these qualities continued to be recognized, especially by the Victorians, as the principle marks of womanliness. Important amongst them was the role of the lady as wife, mother, and mistress of a household.

Feminism, the advocacy of equality and, more important, lack of distinction between the sexes, further rejected the roles to which women had previously aspired. The equality for which the feminist definition of women aimed through the introduction of co-educational and co-residential schemes has actually been undermined by it. The failure to distinguish the sexes allows men in many situations to dominate women through their naturally more forceful, aggressive and physically dominant characteristics. Yet despite the refusal of the chattering classes to subscribe to the traditional, if vague, definition of the lady used by Austen and others, the notion remains remarkably strong. It is well understood by the vast majority of ordinary people, who have no difficulty in assessing the appropriateness of the title for women of their acquaintance.

The mutual respect indicated by manners depends upon a shared moral vocabulary — as literature demonstrated until recently

The idea of community is one which can only exist when individuals can meet with an expectation of shared values. The spontaneity of individuals is possible only when it is recognized that unlimited self-satisfaction cannot be achieved. The protection of individual freedom lies in the knowledge that other, stronger, individuals cannot dominate weaker members of society.

There is an old dispute about whether rules restrict action or allow freedom. Professor George Martin takes it up. Both manners and language, whether it is written or spoken, have in common an agreed set of rules, or 'grammar'. Writers such as Shaw have mocked these rules as artificial. The more perceptive writers, such as Robert Frost, have seen that without common languages and rules, reading and writing are impossible, and so are deep truths about human nature. Speaking properly, and acting properly, are not new ideas. The knowledge that manners foster areas of shared humanity was already present as far back as the work of Homer. And the Greek reverence for hospitality which survived in literature through to Dante and beyond is one of the key building blocks of civilization.

Society requires spiritual discourse, not merely the political relationships described by Plato and Aristotle. Christian notions, such as charity, helped to encourage such virtues through advocacy of courtly behaviour. In later writers, particularly the novelists of the nineteenth century, good speech, writing and behaviour are usually taken to indicate good character. The shared moral vocabulary described by Professor Martin and many of the other authors is precisely what makes for an orderly society. Without the communication it makes possible, society becomes meaningless and ungovernable. Curiously, without order and artifice, there is neither spontaneity nor expression.

Developing appropriate manners depends upon learning from one's elders — and on their behaving with maturity and common sense

This spontaneity, which a broad set of rules allows, rather than prevents, is identified by many of the authors as a key quality which manners helps to foster. It is also why people of different status, income and — as Professor Anthony O'Hear's chapter points out — generation, were able to engage in social discourse. Deference to, and respect for, older people spring from a natural recognition of the different behaviours suitable for different stages of life. The behaviour suitable for each generation allowed for some of the natural inclinations of people of that age. What was more important, however, was respect and allowance for those of other ages. The manners of the young included not only respect for their elders, but allowed for youthful enquiry and exuberance. The outward appearance of maturity in older people, on the other hand, should give way naturally to the wisdom and acceptance of mortality and old age. And did so until the advent of the 'middle-aged trendy'.

Following such manners promoted a framework of orderly behaviour rather than chaotic self-indulgence. When a later generation abandoned such manners as 'repressive' or 'bad faith' it gave itself up to a selfishness unlimited by thought for others. That sort of selfishness, in fact, makes everyone less free. Egalitarianism and impulse, which then corrode the ease which manners protect, have always, unfortunately, appealed to the young. But that makes it all the more important that older people should, by example, demonstrate their undesirability and unworkability.

The cult of youth is a symptom of an arrested moral development, obvious in the outward signals of careless and intimidating clothing

The cult of youth widespread since the 1960s is especially damaging; those, no longer young, who cling foolishly to the attitudes and behaviour of the young deprive others of exemplars of suitable behaviour. The indulgence of youth removes the framework for discourse between people of different ages, and ultimately deprives society of any models for acceptance of the basic principles of civilized life. The young adopting an affectation of maturity may deprive a few individuals of some of the experiences of adolescence and early adulthood; adults trying to ape teenagers ultimately deny the dignity, precepts, and mature judgement appropriate to their age.

Common sense tells us that people *do* judge by appearances. Often they have no time to do anything else. What else can they rely on, particularly in casual encounters? Dress then is not just private preference, but a way people show outwardly what their concerns and attitudes are, especially towards other people. The current enthusiasm for clothes which are utilitarian, aggressively intimidatory or openly sexual indicates a contempt for culture and a rejection of aesthetic and moral concern for others.

In her chapter, Dr Athena Leoussi describes clothes — one of the most visible examples of the cult of youth — as an outward expression of the personality of both the times and the wearer. The bewildering variety of styles of dress seen today includes a number which seem actively in favour of anarchic extremes. The fashions of the gang might have been specially designed to intimidate. The popularity of jeans among modern city dwellers is not because they are suitable for heavy manual work. Most have no involvement in such jobs. What it reflects is a view of life which recognizes only limited physical needs and aspirations. Wearing exercise clothes outside the gym indicates an unhealthy obsession with health. The attempt to claim that all bodies are equally attractive leads to shapeless and shabby neglect of appearance.

The desire to dress appropriately indicates self-restraint and a recognition of one's effect on others. Some modern clothes, however, seem to express sexual or violent attitudes. Overtly sexual clothing undermines the privacy which sexuality ought to have. 'Unisex' fashions erode the normal structure of relations between men and women.

Learning the rules of fair play: competition and sportsmanship can be one way of inculcating courteous behaviour in the young
Dr Simon Green, rather than addressing another instance of manners, analyses a way in which they can be learnt. Traditions of sportsmanship and fair play have always been connected with manners — tennis players at Wimbledon are more likely to be penalized for bad language than for a foul stroke. Both manners and sport are about 'playing the game'. Dr Green finds, indeed, that many of the metaphors for good behaviour — 'playing a straight bat', 'keeping within your crease' — come from cricket which has long been regarded as a sport with a particular tradition of fair play and manners amongst competitors. The values exemplified by cricket were a reflection of common social values the English gentleman upheld, and those values, which led to the universal popularity of the game, were in turn instilled in future generations through the game. At a time of social upheaval, the cricketing ethos provided a shared set of opinions about acceptable behaviour.

Although a first-class sportsman may need considerable innate talent, it is developed by patience and practice, by recognizing one's limits and deferring to fellow team-mates when necessary. Better competitors often find that some modesty helps their style of play — outright aggression does not lend itself to successful batting, for example. Deference was encouraged not only by recognizing the limits of one's own ability, however, but in the practice of congratulating opposing players on good performances. Co-operation amongst all players was also inculcated by the fact that in cricket many situations arise for which there are no set rules. This sense of fair play extended to the ability — indeed, the duty — of players to overrule an umpire's decision in their favour if they believed themselves to have been in the wrong.

The *cause celèbre* of a sporting scandal can provide an example of the importance which was attached to 'fair play'; and the row which surrounds it can teach valuable lessons in what constitute good manners, and of the importance of a gentleman's reputation, judgment, and willingness to apologize for his mistakes. The teaching of cricket

— as the game used to be — shows how manners can be succinctly and explicitly taught rather than just evolve.

Manners enable easy relations between those from different backgrounds and ranks: they can bind societies which appear impossible to reconcile

The universal adoption of values of fair play and manners may not (difficult though English readers may find it to believe) depend entirely on a passion for cricket. But the shared view of correct behaviour so many of the authors see as essential can create orderly societies from unpromising material. Professor Shelton Reed looks at the example of the Southern states of the USA, where people from very different backgrounds were able to live and work together by adhering to a set of manners. These Southern manners are seen by some as too friendly or over-expressive. Part of their charm is their emphasis on such things as flirting or deferring. This can lead to occasional misunderstandings when compliments are taken too literally or to mistrust when they are thought hypocritical. They are, however, entirely appropriate for the problems, concerns and social order of the Southern states. Their impact as a cohesive force in an area of widespread racial and social diversity has been compared in influence with the effects of the Civil War. In particular, the respect — which might elsewhere seem somewhat exaggerated — present in so many Southern greetings was an essential tool for making conversation possible; smoothing inequalities of race, wealth and social position in an exceptionally varied arena.

The 'democratic' nature of the manners of the South is in essence one of familiarity. The kind of familiarity which might seem ostentatious or presumptuous elsewhere was prized in close-knit communities. Indeed, many Southern firms operate rather like extended families, and outsiders can alienate Southern employees with behaviour which would be unremarkable elsewhere. By a respectful treatment of his fellows as brothers, the Southern novelist Owen Wister pointed out, the Southern gentleman, if he merited it, would quickly gain their acknowledgement of him as a superior.

Manners offer more than a stylish gloss to behaviour, and can, in some communities, be essential to the community's work

Dr Robert Grant argues that all civilized societies find that manners make things very much easier. But there are some communities where manners do not only make life more stylish and pleasant. They are essential. In academic life, the pursuit of truth ought to be the chief purpose of all the members of the community. Tolerance and good manners are vital to ensure that a proper atmosphere for debate is maintained. Rival claims can then be subjected to analysis by reason and, in the case of science, experimental tests.

Yet, Dr Grant points out, this atmosphere, essential to the pursuit of truth, has been undermined by the denial, particularly by many literary critics, of such a thing as objective truth. Other subjects have been compromised by the political concerns of those who dominate the field. Those who have a political axe to grind undermine free expression and debate by preventing other ideas from being tested. The study of AIDS, Dr Grant believes, has been hindered and cramped by the refusal to acknowledge evidence which might offend particular interest groups. The desire of many scholars to avoid appearing illiberal, meanwhile, makes it easy for radicals to hijack university committees and appointment boards. A respect for truth demands respect for, and manners toward, those who serve it.

Abandoning respect and courtesy can prevent discourse, not only in the academy, but in any professional encounter

The search for truth in diagnosis or advice with problems which Dr Bruce Charlton examines in the realm of professionals' relationships with clients, also relies upon the notion of respect. It is about keeping one's distance; knowing one's place. Behaviour which might be appropriate between friends is not always useful between bank manager and customer or doctor and patient. The job which professionals have to do makes our relations with them different. A doctor who has to diagnose a patient's disease may find it more difficult in the atmosphere which might suit two friends having dinner. A recognition that people cannot be equal, at least in the roles which they perform in society, and that their positions should affect behaviour toward them, and their behaviour toward others, is a cornerstone of social relations which manners recognized and helped to hold in place.

The clumsiness of rules and charters designed to replace manners

The use of first names, or false chumminess, can make it difficult for patients and doctors to maintain an effective relationship. The assault of lapel badges which declare the wearer's political allegiances, or walls covered with hectoring posters in a waiting room, can also make relations more difficult for professionals and those who consult them. Without these roles being acknowledged by both parties, it is inevitable that a slew of charters, contracts and resorts to litigation will develop. They are no substitute for manners, but their clumsy mechanisms are the only alternative to chaos when manners are abandoned.

These clumsy rules, rather than natural manners, are now commonplace. Yet 'big' solutions, implemented by codes, are no answer to the flexibility of small habits. Many of the authors point out that although manners are small in themselves, that is part of their strength. By practising them daily, they become second nature. Professor Michael Aeschliman examines problems of crime and civic breakdown and finds that the abandonment of manners and habits — the small things progressives are eager to disregard in their search for large underlying explanations — is in fact the most likely basis for this collapse. Life is not founded upon large sociological theses or unadulterated rational analysis. Manners and courtesy may be minor matters, but only in the sense that they are incessant, habitual actions which do not attract much notice. These habits can only be ingrained in the family.

The ingrained habits which can foster manners are best developed in the home. Domestic solutions to social disorder may be more important than political ones

The daily routines of polishing shoes, writing thank you letters, deferring to adults and strangers, are what fosters the disciplines of self-control, consideration and courtesy which will later allow easy and civilized societies. What is more, Professor Aeschliman argues, they can solve or lessen large problems for individuals. Depression or misfortune in life can often be mitigated by the mere routine of daily life. 'Keeping going', and without inconveniencing others, is something which is taught best by the drill of chores and the family routine. Huxley's vision in *Brave New World* of the abandonment of the family, and the replacement of its ingrained disciplines by large systems which can make people good, is a chilling sight of the natural outcome of those progressive theories which argue that the family is an unimportant element in moral order. In fact, the way the family instills order and concern for truth, courtesy and deference may make it one of the only remaining institutions which offers any hope against the collapse of civilization.

But can manners work in societies with no shared values?

As Professor Tristram Engelhardt establishes in the final chapter, the thin platitudes which pass for a shared world culture, with no appeal to authority beyond the participants, are bound to lead to collapse, or clumsy rules and prohibitions. One of the chief obstacles to the regeneration of manners is this relativism of modern society, particularly obvious in the cosmopolitan city. Without a shared central set of values, manners become something which can as easily offend as compliment. But their replacement, the linguistic dogmas of the politically correct lobby, cannot provide trust. That was present in relations between those who shared good manners, not because they were compelled to follow them by rules, but because it was natural and habitual to do so.

Rule book manners are little better than politically correct codes

The idea of manners as instinctive, ingrained by routines taught in the family, runs through many of the chapters in this volume. An adherence to what is appropriate, depends, as several authors stress, not upon the rote learning of guides to etiquette. The forms of etiquette are, of course, known and followed by people possessed of good manners, but manners are more than that. The adoption of correct table manners or forms of address to the various ranks of the aristocracy, Caroline Moore shows, was never enough to create a gentleman. Since manners change with an individual's age, youthful enthusiasm should develop into mature consideration and the wisdom and tolerance of old age. Since manners change from age to age, it is important that the moral values which underpin temporal manners are instilled from generation to generation. While mere observance of form does not constitute good manners, form is important and helpful. The ingrained knowledge of what is courteous and the ways or forms to express it indicate another major quality of manners identified by several authors. Manners are spontaneous and unaffected; although they rely on an appropriate understanding of the station of the participants, and their relations to one another, they have nothing to do with snobbery, or rank alone, but with the ease which springs from trust, predictability and practice.

The spontaneity of manners desirable in itself, but also makes life easier and is part of the route to civilized pleasure

While the authors identify these and other specific examples of difficulties which the decline of manners has created, it may leave the impression that manners are no more than the tools of a useful system for easing social discourse. The failure of politically correct language and regulation to protect citizens' rights, it might be argued, does not mean that any system, if effective would be as good as any other. But even if manners were not functional, it could still be said that they are a good thing in themselves: those who continue to practice courtesy may now often have their actions misunderstood, but their behaviour is clearly preferable to that of those who do not follow their example.

Nor are manners simply a matter of dour puritanical morality. Their capacity for reining in anti-social or selfish impulses does not lead to a dull or oppressive society, but is an essential part of allowing the development of refined pleasure. It is no coincidence that the most visible manners are the rituals associated with eating, drinking, smoking, dress and conversation — not in a bid to stifle these pleasures, but in order that they can be enjoyed properly, with the ease and cultured appreciation which civilized societies and individuals might expect as natural and instinctive.

1

Being a Gentleman

Manners, Independence and Integrity

Caroline Moore

The Gentleman today: seen as chinless wonder or brainless snob

What is a 'gentleman'? No one under 50 would use the term without the face-saving gracelessness of those inverted commas: at best, they suggest a hedge of self-conscious irony; more usually, they signal a simple sneer. The popular view of a gentleman is poised somewhere between the imbecile parasite and the villainous one: between Wooster-esque chinless wonders, and those heartless capitalist toffs who are as much the stock-in-trade of television now as wicked baronets once were of Victorian melodrama.

This is nothing new. The gentleman has always been the target for hatred, ridicule and contempt, the satirist's Aunt Sally. In 1846, Nathanial Hawthorne produced a particularly fine satire upon the very notion of a 'fine gentleman'. What makes 'Feathertop' so disturbing is that it exploits the dismay that all of us sometimes feel in the presence of a being clothed in the impervious mask of merely conventional good manners.

'Feathertop' is a scarecrow, simulcrum. He is made of a withered pumpkin, old sticks and ancient, ragged clothes. A New England witch constructs him, breathes life into him with her clay pipe, and sends him forth to dazzle the locals and seduce a merchant's pretty daughter. A fine gentleman, this fable implies, is a diabolical stuffed shirt. His rank and nobility are only sustained by the ignorant willingness of ordinary people to be duped; in fact, the animated version is of less use than a plain scarecrow. And the most seductive of the arts of this illusion is his 'perfect witchery of well-ordered manners'.

At first, the gentleman-scarecrow produces only the simplest formulaic responses, 'Really! Indeed! Pray tell me! Is it possible! Upon my word! By no means! O! Ah! Hem!'; but soon it can turn a threadbare compliment; then, as it transmutes into 'a thorough and practised man of the world, systematic and self-possessed', his manners become a triumph of artifice:

> Nothing had been left rude or native in him; a well-digested conventionalism had incorporated itself thoroughly with his substance and transformed him into a work of art. Perhaps it was this peculiarity that invested him with a species of ghastliness and awe.[1]

Manners are mere artifice; the social being, whose nature is formed by 'conventionalism', is a mere automaton. The implicit ideals — the puritan-Romantic ones of individuality, spontaneity and sincerity — are asocial. In Hawthorne's fable, only a child and a dog see through the imposture.

Artificiality of manners seen as self-denial and cowering to authority

This puritan-Romantic mix is still potent. The world is still consistently seen in terms of dichotomies: the individual and society, inner and outer, appearance and reality, freedom and constraint, spontaneity and artifice, creativity and conventionality, originality and respectability, self-fulfilment and morality, rebellion and stultification.

In the last 30 years, however, a bleakly deterministic strand of thought has threatened to become dominant. It sometimes melds with the old rebellious-progressive outlook, though it is in many ways its antithesis. Romanticism proclaims the supreme value of the self; radical modern determinism asserts that even the self is a 'bourgeois' illusion. Where they meet is in the common human sense of being trapped.

Old-fashioned Romantics championed personal freedom and political revolt against the tyranny of authority; the frustration of these dreams created disillusionment and despair. A strong sense of bitterness, powerlessness and betrayal are at the root of post-romanticism, modernism, nihilism and all the other dehumanizing 'isms' that follow in its wake.

The modern version of this creed of powerlessness and despair has gained a remarkable currency. Its success in infiltrating our everyday thought and speech is comparable to that of Freudianism. Everybody can now talk glibly about 'repression' and 'complexes', believes in the 'unconscious', and 'knows' that infant traumas can cripple the adult mind, without having read a word of psychoanalytic theory. Similarly, talk of 'conditioning', or of being the 'product' of an 'environment', is now endlessly bandied.

Such ideas became current towards the end of the 1960s, which witnessed an extraordinary explosion of theories and theorists. They were often loosely grouped together as 'structuralists', and were even more loosely Marxist in their outlook. Their influence spanned academic disciplines, leaping like a forest fire across history, linguistics, anthropology, psychology, literary criticism and philosophy. Since every group — like revolutionaries throughout history — constantly splintered with accusations of bad faith, generalizations are difficult; but structuralists (though many rejected this label) shared a common belief that human actions are explained and determined by deep structures, systems or encoded forces — linguistic, cultural, economic, political ('power structures'), psychoanalytical, socio-anthropological — below the surface, always unrecognized or unconscious, and so beyond the control of individual conscious decisions, which they not merely influence but create. The human individual becomes passive: 'men and women' are no longer 'subjects of their history'.

E P Thompson sums up this passive mood in his attack on the new-wave Marxism: in the world of this new ideology

> We are *structured* by social relations, *spoken* by pre-given linguistic structure, *thought* by ideologies, *dreamed* by myths, *gendered* by patriarchal sexual norms, *bonded* by affective obligations, *cultured* by *mentalités* and *acted* by history's script. None of these ideas is, in origin, absurd, and some rest upon substantial additions to knowledge. But all slip, at a certain point, from sense to absurdity, and, in their sum, all arrive at a common terminus of unfreedom.[2]

Individuality seen as impossible against societal conditioning

In the structuralist world, there is no space for human aspirations or emotions, for creativity, spontaneity or even individuality. We are all scarecrow automatons. As E P Thompson remarks, this nightmare vision is

> the ultimate product of self-alienated reason...in which all human products, endeavours, institutions, and even culture itself, appear to stand *outside* of men, to stand *against* men.

If all men are born in chains, some are axiomatically more enchained than others. Strangely enough, Marxist-feminist intellectuals, and those who profess most loudly that others are ruled by conditioning, assume in practice that they themselves are mysteriously exempt — a paradox like that of Epimenides the Cretan, who affirmed that all Cretans were liars. Conversely, the poor gentleman, governed by a rigid 'exterior' code of manners, cultured by the attitudes of a particular limited class and embedded in an imperialist historical era, is of course triply enslaved.

The spontaneity of the gentleman provides escape from the determinist view of the structuralists

In fact, however, what makes a gentleman enviable is not so much his wealth or birth (a gentleman may well be without the first, and is sometimes not endowed with the second), it is precisely his superior freedom. The gentleman is not the 'product of self-alienated reason': in him, those miserable misconstructed dichotomies between the individual and society, manners and sincerity, tradition and individuality are dissolved. The gentleman is at ease in society: he may be diffident, shy, or even rough-and-ready; but he is never 'alienated'. Society is his element, in which he may be himself. Politeness is no constraint, precisely because the manners or his society are no 'code' but a language, rich, flexible, restrained and infinitely subtle — a tool, not a master, used to express rather than conceal. The gentleman at his best is the triumph of individualism, achieved not in adolescent Romantic solitude, but in the mature moral world of human relationships. For him, 'society' is not an alien abstraction, but a network of obligations between human beings.

Traditions allow the gentleman to move in society rather than be alienated by it

The worst charge which is commonly laid at the gentleman's door — that he respects tradition — is his greatest strength. It does not 'enslave' him to the past and it may liberate him from some of the narrownesses of the present. Nor, of course, does it entail any particular branch of politics. Recognizing the value of the past suggests but does not enforce conservatism; but this is very different from Conservatism. Indeed, awareness of the past will leave no room for doubt that there have been plenty of radical gentlemen, Whig gentlemen, even Dissenting gentlemen (particularly, in Victorian England, among the Unitarians).

The only thing he cannot be is an idealogue, of any persuasion.

Tradition, unlike ideology, can never be a 'trap', if only because it is multi-layered, rich in possibilities: its voice is never single, but, like the sound of a stream, is made up of myriads of different tongues. At times, of course, the babble may sound like confusion; certainly, there are often apparent contradictions within it. Yet, unlike the single inflexibly authoritarian voice of ideology, it can encompass disagreements. They can be discussed, can find a common ground even in the rather gentlemanly art of agreeing to differ, because they share a common language, a sense of a shared history. Tradition is like an endless conversation between different interpretations of the past, and between past and present.

Community and the freedom to act as individuals in it depends upon shared traditions

One is tempted, here, to try to resurrect the word 'conversation' in its old sense: like 'manners', it used to have a wider social meaning. 'Conversation' was more than social chit-chat: it could mean 'society', 'intimacy' and 'intercourse' (in all senses of that much narrowed term); it meant 'the action of consorting or having dealings with others', and it could be used to express a sense of belonging (as in the Biblical 'Our conversation is in heaven'). What we would nowadays call a sense of community is bound up with our ability to talk to each other with a common language — which goes beyond the sharing of mere words, and is a matter of shared traditions, shared assumptions, shared ways of doing things.

For many, this will point to precisely what is objectionable about a gentleman. His class is like a club; his manners are exclusive. They are designed to make sure that those who do not share his assumptions and background have no access to his privileges. The language of good manners, in this view, only reinforces 'oppressive power structures'.

The gentleman in Kingsley and Gissing: two novelists who view membership through manners, not money

Naturally, there is a certain amount of truth in this. There is eloquent testimony in life and literature to just this sense of exclusion. In Charles Kingsley's passionate radical novel, *Yeast*, the gamekeeper Tregarva, who is in love with a lady, laments

Ah, sir, I see it now, as I never did before, what a wall all these

> little defects build up round a poor man…Let the rich be as rich as they will. I, and those like me, covet not money, but manners.[3]

This sense of exclusion is usually felt with most bitterness and longing by those clinging on the fringes of the middle-classes, like that most class-conscious of novelists, George Gissing. They are, in the wonderfully suggestive title of his most famous novel, *Born in Exile*.

Yet throughout history, the notion of a gentleman has been far from class-bound and far from rigid. Tradition once again offers a liberal flexibility. Gentlemen do not and never have come out of one mould. Though I have suggested that they may share, through their language of manners, a certain *way* of doing things, this is not at all the same as saying that they will all act the same, all do the same things.

Here, indeed, the very richness of the material creates problems. If one is to answer the question 'what is a gentleman?', one will have to recognize that not only are there many varieties of gentlemen within any age, but that ideas about gentlemanliness shift and reshape in emphasis from age to age (though the gentleman shapes as well as is shaped by them). To trace the changes from medieval 'gentilesse' through the literature of the Renaissance courtier to the modern gentleman is not within the scope of this chapter. I will therefore be concentrating chiefly upon the Victorian gentleman, since this is the era which has shaped our present rigid caricatures most strongly.

The Victorian gentleman: a notion based upon behaviour rather than wealth or rank

Many of our modern stereotypes are far too inflexibly narrow. The notion of a gentleman is peculiarly free-floating — which is why so many Victorians remarked that it was impossible to define, though they knew one when they met him. First, of course, it is not confined to any specific rank or class. The early use of the word, as Shirley Robin Letwin pointed out in her excellent study of *The Gentleman in Trollope*, indicated no particular social class, but simply meant 'freeman'. In its subsequent development the title flourished

> just because it had nothing to do with "class", as defined by birth, occupation, wealth or rank.[4]

Though theoretically justifiable, 'nothing' is in practice an exaggeration. Certainly the ordinary presumption used to be that those of exalted birth and rank would be likely to be gentlemen. Maintaining their claim to that title, however, depended solely upon their conduct, as foreigners often remarked with surprise. According to Madame de Staël,

> You will often hear it said, even by persons of the lower class, "Though he be a lord, he is not a gentleman".[5]

The free-floating status of the gentleman was partly a reaction to the relative fluidity of English society. If the 'class-system' is a 'trap', it is one which large portions of the population spent considerable and successful effort and ingenuity in evading. 'Social mobility', as Letwin observed, is 'an old English pastime'.

The independent status of a gentleman was partly asserted as a conservative reaction to this fluidity. It could be consoling, if your impoverished monarch were selling off peerages and knighthoods (for which James I charged £40) to repeat the adage that though a king could make a lord, he could not make a gentleman. But it was also radical. Even a man who could not afford those 40 pounds could be a truer gentleman than the king.

According to F Wills in his Victorian *Lay Sermons*, this made the title both peculiarly exclusive, and peculiarly democratic:

> The word "gentleman" expressed the highest standard of courage and truth, courtesy and honour. It was a word in the superlative degree — no man could be more than a gentleman, and no man, being less, could be a gentleman at all. So that this was a very proud conception, and it made the poorest and most obscure man at his ease amongst the greatest...And this feeling of equality was the origin, and caused the development of manners.[6]

The notion of 'gentleman' set standards of acceptability in response to changing class boundaries

Several Victorian writers claimed that this was the source or a symptom of the peculiar nature of English society, which combines the conservative and the radical, encompasses stability and change, and makes its revolutions Glorious and Bloodless. G P Marsh, in his *Lectures in the English Language*, believed that the concept of a gentleman was so English as to be 'essentially untranslatable'. This is because

> It was in England that the ideal of social grace and moral excellence in man, as attributes of humanity superior in worth to the artificial

> claims of rank and conventional manner, was first conceived, named and realized.[7]

A contributor to *The Spectator* in 1901 similarly claimed that our language made manifest 'the glory of the English nation', for in England the derivations of 'gentillesse'

> soon altered their meaning...and gave us the significance of "gentle" — the very antithesis of pride of race and arrogance of blood.

This is in contrast to the class-bound rigidities of the French system:

> The French preserved the "true" meaning of the word *gentil-homme*, and its preservation may in a sense be said to have produced the Revolution.[8]

But if a gentleman is not necessarily a man of rank, wealth, or birth, what is he? He is, according to many Victorians, merely the repository of all those moral excellences which *used* to be associated with the aristocracy. This, however, does not help very much: the descriptions of a gentleman elicited by this high-minded and very Victorian definition tend to be a mere conglomeration of excellencies, a chivalric-Aristotelian-Christian hybrid of often contradictory perfections. He is brave and tender, self-abnegating and fired by self-respect, strictly honourable and infinitely tolerant, generous and prudent...He is apt to be a plaster saint, animated by a sublime benevolence which is a sentimentalized Christianity.

The gentleman's sense of respect for rank subordinate to notion of self-respect

It is more interesting to look at the apparent contradictions in the definition, for it is possible to argue either that the gentleman is (poor soul) riddled with post-structuralist contradictions, entrapped in a Quixotically indefensible position, or that he exemplifies an ethos, a way of life which straddles divides, living in the world but not bounded by it. It may be we, the modern critics, who are entrapped by the assumptions of modern 'self-alienated reason'.

Central to the English notion of a gentleman is a certain sort of moral independence, a certain self-reliance and integrity — fostered, perhaps, by our island's long Protestant history, with its emphasis upon the primacy of the individual conscience. This is in one sense highly and acceptably democratic: in the 'class-bound' Victorian society, a humble country doctor, descended from a line of honest squires, would never doubt that he was the moral equal of a duke.

However, such a statement has several important qualifications, which deflect its radical implications. This doctor would, as a matter of manners and possibly conviction, pay deference to the duke's rank — not in abject servility, but with a respect that is bound up with self-respect. He is discharging a social obligation, and expects due consideration in return.

Moreover, he may respect an ancient lineage because his own sense of himself is bound up with his own family history. Trollope's Dr Thorne is the example here: he has no noble blood, but prides himself upon his genealogy.

> No man had a stronger theory as to the advantage held by men who have grandfathers over those who have none, or have none worth talking about.

In the novel, Trollope makes it perfectly clear that this is a flaw in his hero. Dr Thorne's 'theory' is too rigid — in its Tory way, too ideological — and threatens human happiness. But he is a useful reminder that family pride, for good and for bad, is not the prerogative of 'the boast of heraldry, the pomp of power'.

Even those progressive Victorians who most resolutely substitute moral worth for social status still often insist upon the influence of good breeding, albeit re-defined. Working class men may well have the requisite family background. As Grant Allen asserts in his novel *Philistia*, a gentleman

> may be the final outcome and efflorescence of many past generations of quiet, unobtrusive, working-man culture.[9]

The effortless sense of what is appropriate natural to the true gentleman

The proliferation of Victorian writings upon the subject highlight the apparent contradictions within the tradition: birth and breeding both are, and are not, important in the make up of a 'true gentleman'. This corresponds to a profound ambiguity about the role of effort in his morality. A gentleman is born, not made — whether born to rank, or one of 'nature's gentlemen'. And even the most democratic of definitions are apt to assert both necessary moral strenuousness, and the impossibility of achieving gentlemanliness by effort alone; simply because nature's gentlemen are, above all else, natural.

If a gentleman were a product, if his conduct involved only the mastering of a set of exterior rules, then it might indeed by possible to 'make' oneself a gentleman by effortful application, a sort of social swotting. But to the gentleman, who bows to no rules from a culture exterior to himself, such efforts can only be the mark of hypocrisy. They signal only social climbing, a false gentleman — a snob.

The true mark of a gentleman, it is widely agreed, is spontaneity. He is frank, natural, unaffected. Tom Jones, for all his rakish flaws, is self-evidently more of a gentleman than the calculating hypocrite Blifil. Generosity and spontaneity are part and parcel of a largeness of heart which overflows mere forms — and which even forgives Blifil at the end of the novel. The gentleman is never a sterile precisionist. 'By a thorough contempt of little excellencies' according to Steele, 'he is master of them...his negligence is unaffected'.[10]

Notoriously, Chesterfield outraged this deeply cherished belief in the importance of natural, honest frankness as the mark of a gentleman. The openness of Chesterfield's gentleman is mere seeming: 'a frank, open and ingenuous exterior, with a prudent and reserved interior', where the 'seeming natural openness' is merely a ploy to put others off their guard. Chesterfield's *Letters*, according to Dr Johnson, 'teach the morals of a whore, and the manners of a dancing master'.[11]

The gentleman, it seems, must be both polished and natural; both born and made; both civilized and spontaneous. And nowhere is this apparent ambiguity towards the civilized and merely acquired social graces more apparent than in the copious literature on the manners of a gentleman.

Although manners natural in a gentleman, it is not adhering to them which creates one

Good manners both are, and are not, vital to a gentleman. 'A Gentleman without manners', as one seventeenth century writer put it, 'is like a custard of addle egges, in a silver coffin'.[12] Yet, as a nineteenth century essayist asserts,

> We must, all of us, know men whose manners leave very much to desire, and yet to whom it would be impossible to refuse the title. A finished gentleman such an one may not be, but a gentleman notwithstanding.[13]

Fine manners, in fact, are not 'part of his actual nature and substance'.

Certainly, too great an attention to etiquette is a sure sign of the false gentleman, as Thackeray claims:

> It is your parvenu who stickles most for what he calls the genteel, and has the most squeamish abhorrence for what is frank and natural.[14]

A particularly good distinction between the manners of the true and the false gentleman is given by a Maori chieftain to Bishop Selwyn.

> The New Zealander, in response to the query as to what he understood by a gentleman, replied "Gentleman gentleman never mind what he does, but piggy gentleman very particular".[15]

Good manners, it seems, are essential to the gentleman, yet not of his essence. The contradiction, however, is perhaps only apparent. It would offer few problems to the Victorians, nurtured in the understanding of Protestant paradox. Manners were to the Victorians like good works, which were essential to salvation, yet not of its essence. Christians are saved by faith alone, and good works performed without faith are worse than useless — they entrap in mere form, in hypocritical self-righteousness; they are artificial, 'dead', the letter of the law. Yet faith, if it have not works, is equally 'dead': a living faith almost necessarily issues forth into good deeds. Similarly — and the analogy is constantly drawn, implicitly and explicitly — good manners are nothing in themselves. 'Outward' manners, according to W R Browne, are only the 'visible sign' of 'those inward manners which make the man'.[16] Mere outward manners deteriorate into mere etiquette, mere formality, foolish prescriptions. Observing the letter of social laws never gains the freedom of the true gentleman, but only entraps one in mere gentility.

The rules of manners give forms of behaviour but not actions through which knowledge of them is shown

This awareness that to talk of 'good manners' may encompass either true courtesy, or the perfect by freeing punctiliousness of the 'piggy gentleman', or slavish aping by the vulgar, is highly Victorian. It should qualify any belief that Victorian society was peculiarly rule-ridden. Andrew St George, in his wide-ranging study, *The Descent of Manners*, which is full of good things, tends to this theory:

> Mid-Victorian behaviour, manners, etiquette and the beliefs which lay beneath them were all about following rules.[17]

Part of his evidence for this is the extraordinary proliferation of self-help guides to good manners. This, however, is one mid-Victorian reaction to the phenomenon:

> If you cling unflinchingly to the etiquette books and Islingtonian formulae, you will often excite a smile as an amusing specimen of affectation.[18]

If you believe, as St George does, that 'manners are social control self-imposed, and etiquette is class control exercised', you may see this as merely the closing of ranks against the swotting parvenu. Yet it also contains a real truth. Good manners have to be more than mere rules and rote.

An etiquette book will tell you that it is correct to write a letter of condolence to an acquaintance whose wife has died. Yet if you merely copied out a specimen of this admittedly difficult art, you would automatically be at fault: the best condolences, like the best manners, are creative, personal, arising out of individual circumstances, tender towards particular susceptibilities, and can never be a matter of 'prescriptive patterns', Good manners are, as Professor Mahaffy remarked of good conversation in 1887, 'a Protean impalpable acquirement', not a rigid code.

Changes in detail do not alter the essence of good-mannered behaviour

Nevertheless, St George is undoubtedly right to point to the extraordinary intricacies of Victorian social etiquette as something remarkable and significant. Astonishingly elaborate conventions governed the now forgotten procedures of exchanging visiting cards (who now knows the significance of bending the corner of the card one leaves in the hall?). You could be judged by whether you ate your fish with a piece of bread, as was correct; or whether you parted your coat tails behind when you sat down, which wasn't; or whether your fork had three prongs or four, upon which the jury was still out.

Most gentlemen would recognize that such prescriptions alter from age to age: 'what are called good manners...contain an element which is transitory, conventional, capricious...' Yet the gentleman will, upon the whole (though circumstances will always alter cases, for the gentleman should never be pedantic, ideological or inflexible) observe such merely conventional proprieties as a matter of course — wherever the letter does not infringe upon the spirit of courtesy.

> The Gentleman does not show his nature by rejecting or disregarding those decencies and proprieties which only belong to this evanescent condition, but by wearing them easily. The ceremonies and etiquette of society are much like our clothes, not of our essence, nor to last beyond this state. But while the need for them does last, the thing is to wear them as though natural to us, and not as though a restraint.[19]

Many, perhaps most gentlemen would be unable to say why they should observe merely trivial 'outward' manners. Yet because his morality is largely unreflective, part of his 'second nature', does not mean that the gentleman's stance is morally negligible — even if he is occasionally found dressing for dinner in the depths of the jungle. There are plenty of theoretical justifications around for observing the merely conventional rules of politeness — particularly from the eighteenth century, with its post-Civil War awareness of the fragility of human civilized values.

Such observances offer cohesion:

> Good manners are to particular societies what good morals are to society in general, their cement and their security.[20]

The purpose of manners chiefly to ease not stifle relations between people

Eighteenth-century justifications emphasize 'ease' rather than morality as the prime benefit of ordinary politeness; and sometimes suggest that it is prompted by prudence rather than charity. According to Swift,

> Good manners is the art of making those people easy with whom we converse.

Its conventions are not alien to human reason, but are the product of it, and offer a useful short-cut for the less talented:

> ...good sense is the principle foundation of good manners, but because the former is a gift which very few among mankind are possessed of, therefore all the civilisations of the world have agreed upon fixing some rules upon common behaviour best suited to

> their general customs or fancies, as a kind of artificial good sense, to supply the defects of nature.[21]

For Dr Johnson, politeness is a 'fictitious benevolence' (not a 'lie', any more than a work of art is a 'lie'):

> ...it supplies the place of it among those who see each other only in public, or but little depend on it.[22]

In these circumstances, of course, faking true friendship would be real hypocrisy.

The 'hypocrisy' of manners actually a way of engendering trust and a deeper honesty in behaviour

Politeness is useful precisely because it both is and isn't believed. No puritan dichotomies between sincerity and lies, inner and outer, are relevant in the usual course of things. Writing 'your humble servant' at the foot of a challenge is not a 'breach of the truth', Chesterfield wrote, because no one believes it:

> they are universally agreed upon, and understood, to be things of course.[23]

As with many of Chesterfield's formulations, this makes the convenances sound empty if useful, necessary manipulations which are seen as such by the gentleman in the know. They are 'necessary guards of the decency and peace of society'.

But it is just as important that politeness is as well as that it isn't believed, or it will not perform this task. The reception of such conventional gestures needs to be polite. And though politeness need not be believed, it is, however, extremely impolite to disbelieve it. Professions of Johnsonian benevolence need to be taken on trust.

Trust — of an undemanding but significant kind — fills up the spaces in those empty social forms. Any speaker acts in trust that he will be rightly understood; any hearer trusts that he shares the same understanding of the words used: 'We could not understand language', as the critic William Empson remarked, 'unless we were always floating in a general willingness to make sense of it.'[24] The trust evoked in an exchange of merely conventional politenesses is peculiarly free-floating: the words themselves hardly mean anything at all. What they express is a sort of trust in trust, a general and shared willingness to understand.

They are perhaps merely 'surface-charity', but they may signal the true bonds of society.

Spontaneous manners of the gentleman are outward demonstration of Christian charity

If the eighteenth century tends to stress the importance of 'surface-charity', the Victorians regularly insist that 'manners spring from the heart'. The final source of all good manners is inward charity — or Charity, for this is usually an explicitly Christian ethos. It is regularly asserted that to be a Christian is to be a true gentleman. *John Halifax, Gentleman* expresses the sentiments of many when John's wife exclaims, 'a Christian only can be a true gentleman'.[25]

To our modern eyes, this is at least faintly ridiculous. It is easier to imagine the Prince of Darkness to be a gentleman than Jehovah (which is why Max Beerbohm enjoys himself portraying the Devil as not-quite-the-thing in 'Enoch Soames'). But the Victorians acknowledged no problem. There is only one perfect gentleman:

> Lord Badlesmere walked slowly up to Tom and laid his hand on his shoulder. "There never was but one *perfect* gentleman since the world began," he said solemnly, "and He was the Son of God".[26]

No matter that one cannot imagine Christ as a comfortable companion at the Victorian dinner table, or that many of His remarks hardly promoted 'ease'. To the Victorians, such objections would be of the letter, rather than of the spirit.

After Christ, Paul is the foremost candidate. 'St Paul was always such a *gentleman*', remarked Lord Carnarvon. Henry Friswell agreed: 'St Paul, in his speech and letters, is the very model of a gentleman...'[27] And the Bible, according to Mary Linskell, is the only perfect 'pocket-book of etiquette': those raised upon it 'shall be at a loss in no good society'.[28]

'Christian' manners adopted by the gentleman allow him to govern himself by being governed by them

When one has finished smiling at the idea of turning to St Paul for advice about fish-knives, however, one is left with the less patronizing realization that Christianity offered to the Victorians an ethos, simultaneously dogmatic and open to infinite individual interpretations, which enabled them to view both gentlemen and their manners in a double perspective. This, though it may lead to confusion, is a tribute to just those interpretative powers of the human mind which, with their creative flexibility, enable it to escape entrapment in its own creations. Good manners are trivial yet important, for they are, though contingently, bound up with the social morality of an age. The Victorians knew and lamented the changing definition of 'manners': that eighteenth-century narrowing of the word, from one which could include a general moral code, a customary or cultural way of life, an ethos, to mere politeness or etiquette. Yet this did not narrow their own definitions: they both accepted and, with evangelical fervour, saw beyond the standard meaning of their time.

This view of the Victorians axiomatically offers no easy prescriptions to solve any putative decline in modern manners; but neither will it allow any easy despair. Certainly, the values of Victorian middle-class society may seem lost for ever: when St George writes that all those etiquette books 'were the surest evidence of class emulation rather than class envy', many will sigh for an innocence irreparably lost. Manners sustain a certain ethos; yet that ethos sustains manners — we cannot now revive the manners without the ethos, or the ethos without the manners. Yet to despair would be to succumb to structuralist logic, which overlooks the possibilities of creative renewal, simply because it discounts the importance of individuality. The Victorian gentleman, who may not control the circumstances which govern his life, but whose self-governing conduct in them creates his moral integrity, ought to be a constant reminder of our human potentialities.

2

Being a Lady

The Protection of Courtesy

Rachel Trickett

Appellation 'lady' now trivialised and unfashionable
People of my generation — born between 1920 and 1925 — well remember an age when the terms Ladies and Gentlemen were common usage. There were 'Ladies Only' compartments on trains; public lavatories were invariably marked 'Ladies' and 'Gentlemen'; in fact any places where the sexes might be segregated were designated in this way. It stopped — fairly abruptly in my recollection — in the 1960s, and since then has been almost completely lost to common usage, except in a few formal announcements; proposals of a toast, for example, or introductions of a star turn in a variety or television show.

At first sight this seems entirely reasonable. The term 'lady', meaning a woman of refined manners, charitable disposition, 'whose manners, habits and sentiments are characteristic of those in the higher ranks of society' is dated in the OED as first used in 1861. 'In modern usage corresponding to gentleman, often merely a courteous synonym for woman'.

Changing views of the 'lady' — from Chaucer to Shakespeare
The durability of the idea of a lady and her behaviour throughout centuries is nowhere better illustrated than by literary example. In the Middle Ages, Chaucer's pilgrims include the wonderfully vocal Wife of Bath who is clearly 'No Lady' and the Prioress whose refinement, delicacy and sensibility are gently mocked but lovingly recorded:

There was also a Nonne, a Prioresse,
That of her smyling was ful simple and coy;

And she was cleped madame Eglantyne.
Ful well she song the service divyne,
Entuned in hir nose ful semely...
At mete wel y-taught was she with-alle;
She let no morsel from her lippes falle,
Nor wet hit fingers in her sauces deppe
....
In courteisye was sit ful much her lest,
Her over lippe wyped she so clene
That in her cup was no farthing sene
Of grese, when she dronken had hir droughter
Ful semely after hir met she raughte
And silenly she was of greet disport,
And ful plesaunt and amiable of port,
And peyned hir to countrefete chere
Of court, and been establich of manere,
And to beholden digne of reverence.
But for to speken of hir conscience,
She was so charitable and so pitous
She wolden wepe, if that she saw a mouse
Caught in a trappe, if it were deed or beldde.
Of smale houndes had she, that she fedde,
With rosted flesh or milk and wastel bread.
But sore weep she if oon of hem were dead
Or if men smoot it with a yerde smerte:
And all was conscience and tendere herte.

So, in the fourteenth century, Chaucer's hearers and readers are at once assumed to recognize the characteristic qualities of ladies like Madame Eglantyne, and even to be amused by their attendant dangers of affectation and a too rarefied gentility.

Some two centuries later, Shakespeare's heroines are set off against their more homespun attendants: Portia against Nerissa, Olivia against Marie, Desdemona against Emilia. Their high-spirited wit and independence is of a different order from the quick-witted plotting and counter-plotting of the servant girls. They are notably capable, too, of friendship among themselves — Helena and Hermia (before Puck's meddling), Beatrice and Hero, Rosalind and Celia. Shakespeare's women share qualities of magnanimity, good sense and courage which were to exercise a wider influence on later writers, especially novelists.

Austen's ladies distinguished by character more than rank

It was the late eighteenth century which, in fact, saw a distinct change in the status of women and the social respect paid to them. The upheavals of the Civil War, and the libertine creed of the Restoration wits had made the seventeenth century an uneasy time in which to cultivate further manners, other than those of a small courtly elite. But by the end of that era of comparative peace and prosperity, the eighteenth century, women's intelligence and sensibility began to be openly acknowledged. It was no longer necessary to be a woman of rank to earn the title 'lady'. The blue-stockings held court in their salons, and a group of talented women poets (whose work has been very recently revived and, it must be said, in some quarters overestimated), Ann Seward, Elizabeth Robinson and Charlotte Smith, for example, emerged into immediate popularity.

Jane Austen's novels at the beginning of the nineteenth century reflect this new atmosphere very clearly. It has become instinctive with her to contrast the heroines with the women in the stories who are recognizably not ladies. A lady may be high-spirited and arty like Elizabeth Bennet and Emma Wodehouse, or reticent and self-effacing like Jane Bennet and Anne Elliott, or impoverished, innocent and garrulous like Miss Bates. The idea of the lady has been firmly removed in Jane Austen's novels from that of class or status. Lady Catherine de Bourgh is far from being a lady and the two types can be found in the same family as in the case of the Bennets. What a lady cannot display is the moral stupidity, frivolity and insensitivity of characters like Mrs Bennet and her daughter Lydia, Isabella Thorpe, Lucy Steele or Mrs Elton.

By this stage of the nineteenth century then, an attractive image of warmth, affection and intelligence had begun to characterize the idea of a lady and her conduct. It developed throughout the century, though at least two of the greatest novelists, Scott and Dickens, inhabit a masculine imaginative world which has little room for other than certain stereotypes of femininity. But Meredith, notably in *Diana at the Crossways* and in the figure of Clara Middleton in *The Egoist*, added to the established consensus of the idea of the new woman, willing to defy convention and break rules for what she believes to be the truth. And to this add Henry James in *Portrait of a Lady*, where the figure of

Isobel, the innocent abroad, is of a bold, 'presumptuous' young woman who becomes fascinated by the attractions of the old Europe, and eventually a victim of its corruption. In what James declared to be the central scene of the novel, where Isobel sits brooding silently on the truth that has been gradually revealed to her, she becomes the old adventurous heroine transformed not so much into a victim as into a living instance of the moral intelligence that is the highest good in James's late novels.

The extraordinarily rich and varied literary examples show how poets and novelists have done more — and more effectively — than any conduct book in establishing a pattern of behaviour. It is from them that we infer what constitutes a lady and how we would expect her to behave.

Nineteenth century ideals of the lady diminished by modern lack of interest in moral character

The twentieth century has done little, if anything to add to this idea. In many ways it has diminished and reversed it. Wells and Shaw helped to popularize the image of the 'new woman', but by the 1920s there had been a loss of interest in individual characterization in the novel. 'Don't expect from me "the old stable ego of the character"', wrote Lawrence, and Lawrence's increasing obsession with the 'eternal feminine' was matched by Joyce's Molly Bloom. The question of being a lady or having a code of conduct became, in this context, completely irrelevant. Even Virginia Woolf's most successful characters, Clarissa Dalloway and Mrs Ramsay, are themselves embodiments of their author's own feminine sensibility, and though 'ladies' in the narrow sense, as their creator was, they can't be set up as models or seen as in any sense exemplary.

This process has continued to the present day — a retreat from character in literature which reflects the retreat from courtesy in the undeferential society. But the survival of the great literature of the past guarantees the survival in common consciousness of a 'lady's' way of looking at life and acting — independent, courageous, compassionate and imaginative, virtues which still retain their deep attraction.

Varied uses of the term 'lady' throughout history add to difficulties of defining its characteristics

There was always a greater problem with the use of the word 'lady' than with that of 'gentleman'. The latter, though properly applied in the Middle Ages to a man of gentle birth, one entitled to bear arms, though not noble, was already in Middle English usage 'a man of chivalrous instincts and fine feelings' (OED). No such general imputation of courtesy attached to the term 'lady', as we have seen, until the nineteenth century. The lady (in Old English the loaf kneader) was the head of the household, the provider. By the twelfth century, the term was adopted to mean the beloved one, the paragon, which the Church took over, about the same time, to confer on the Mother of God, mediatrix of all graces, and 'sole of all her sex'. But the problem remained that 'lady' was not only a courtesy title but a genuine title prefixed to the names of the daughters of dukes, marquises and earls. The OED again defines this as 'a less formal substitute for the designation of rank in speaking of a marchioness, countess, viscountess or baroness'. Thus the word inevitably had overtones of aristocratic status as well as its other attributes of mistress, beloved, or woman of refined manners. It is hardly surprising, then, that with the reaction against the 'deferential' society, the whole ethos of courtesy and acceptable conduct, the term should have fallen into disuse in recent years. In fact its gradual demise started much earlier.

The term 'lady' not widely used in Victorian era: qualities of 'the lady' subsumed in definitions of 'womanliness'

It is remarkable that between 1880 and the early years of the twentieth century, woman or girl was more commonly used in what we might call 'conduct books' — for these still remained remarkably popular. Mrs Lynn Lynton's 'The Girl of the Period' (a collection of essays she contributed to *The Saturday Review* in 1883) is dedicated to 'All good girls and true women'. Mrs Lynton doesn't use the term lady or gentlewoman in her chapter on 'Womanliness', but she concludes it with an entirely traditional summary of qualities the nineteenth century valued in 'the lady':

> In a word, the womanly woman whom we all once loved, and in whom we have still a kind of traditional belief, is she who regards the wishes of men as of some weight in female action; who holds to love rather than opposition; to renounce, not defiance; who takes more pride in the husband's fame than in her own; who glories in the protection of his name, and in her state as wife;

> who feels the honour given to her as wife and matron far dearer than any she may earn herself by her personal prowess…

Not a definition likely to recommend itself to today's women, this is an entirely traditional summary of the old idea of the lady under a different verbal guise.

'Manners for Women' recently republished by *Past Times*, again shows the early twentieth century refusal to use the term 'lady', but its conduct advice on matters of etiquette shows it still reflecting a society where the code is both strict and generally accepted. The last example I would give is Mrs Beeton, whose section on 'The Mistress' (I quote from the edition of 1880) concludes:

> Let her prove herself, then, the happy companion of man, and able to take unto herself the praises of the pious prelate, Jeremy Taylor, who says — "A good wife is Heaven's last and best gift to men — his angel and minister of graces innumerable — his gem of many virtues — his casket of jewels — her voice is sweet music — her smiles the brightest day; her kiss the guardian of his innocence; — her arms the pale of his safety, the balm of his health, the balsam of his life; — her industry his sweet wealth — her economy his safest steward; her lips his faithful counsellors; — her bosom the softest pillow of his cares; and her prayers, the ablest advocates of Heaven's blessings on his head".

Mrs Beeton recommends this as the true role of the modern housekeeper.

But, in spite of the useful reminder that simple nomenclature — the dropping of 'lady' for 'girl', 'woman', 'mistress of the household' was happening in the late nineteenth and early twentieth centuries, none of these usages could be accepted, or, to some extent understood, by present day society. It is the purpose of this chapter to try to understand why, and to consider the possible effects of this rejection.

Demise of aspirations to be ladylike abetted by feminism and rejection of defining women in roles as wives or mothers

It was undoubtedly a result of the feminist movement that the notion of a distinction made between the sexes was gradually declared to be inadmissible — the whole concept of the lady — of a 'womanliness' belonging to a patriarchal, male-dominated society, and so ill-suited to a situation where women were as often the breadwinners as men, and more often on their own — single mothers, spinsters or professional women who lived alone or with children and who did not need a male presence in the household (though still expecting male financial support from estranged husbands). This was a perfectly rational interpretation of the increasingly common situation of women.

It happened, also, to coincide with several other movements in society which took encouragement from the feminist attitude. First, the popular idea of co-residence and co-education in schools and universities. All comprehensive schools were co-educational. By the end of the 1980s all Oxford and Cambridge Colleges had gone mixed except for one or two, and Independent Schools had begun to take girls into their sixth forms, or, in some cases, throughout. In such a climate, it was easy for other institutions to introduce a mixed male and female community for different and often less idealistic (or ideological) reasons: mixed wards in general hospitals, for example. Without warning to the public, the sexes were mingled in general wards when it seemed financially easier to fill the beds at once, regardless of what was now called gender. Together with this unisex society came the informality that stemmed from a rejection of deference. Women and men were universally, in hospitals, addressed or referred to, by their Christian names. An assumption of friendliness and general joviality replaced any concept of courtesy. The popular idiom 'I couldn't care less' had become a reality, since 'caring' indicated a profession of experts — the so-called 'caring professions'; social workers and counsellors having taken the place of the older culture of compassion among members of a community or congregation.

Culture of equality and abandonment of distinction between the sexes have failed to advance women's opportunities

This situation was almost universally accepted at the beginning of 1990, but during the following four years, grievance, dissatisfaction and uneasiness began to be felt very forcibly. Attention was centred on the position of women in the universities: they were doing less well than the men. In some mixed colleges, complaints were made not only about sexual harassment, but about a general sense of uneasiness in what seemed still a predominantly male environment. Men, women contended, no longer treated them with respect or courtesy. But these terms had already become meaningless. The only remedies suggested were characterized by a Fellow of Hertford College, Oxford, who felt that women suffered from the 'adversarial' tutorial system and should perhaps be treated differently from men in the Final examinations — a notion that conveniently ignored the reason many men's Colleges originally gave for going co-residential — that the women were getting such excellent results from their single-sex colleges.

The superior results in the school league tables of women's single sex schools gave another impetus to the growing belief that the unisex idea had been a disaster. Feminists began to demand what they had previously fought against — special status, special consideration, a separate identity. But they were too late, the revolution had taken place, and taken over. Men, no longer constrained by any code of conduct, and used, often enough, to a rejection of the old courtesies, reverted to indifference, or increasingly to violence. Domestic violence became common, public violence, often directed against women, a particular source of alarm. The most extraordinary effect of this was that women began to imitate this behaviour. 'Girl gangs' making savage attacks on other women (less often on men) have been much in the news recently, especially an interview with one of the gangsters who, when asked how she looked at her future, said that she knew she couldn't go on being one of a gang when she 'grew up' and declared her ambition 'to become a social worker'. A serious satirist could hardly have got away with this stroke.

Failure to recognize sex distinctions allows male domination through aggression and physical strength

But the situation is inevitably anarchic. When all ideas of a code of conduct collapse, when the concept of courtesy disappears, a condition of primitivism prevails, and its principle is, inevitably, brute force. There is no other way in which to assert some sort of predominance, some sort of pack leadership. And in this situation men will inevitably prevail for the simple, biological reason that they are stronger than women. So that women, without some code of deference or respect, become increasingly victims, however much they try to compete with their superiors in strength. If they can't conquer, they must either submit or demand special status (which the present situation denies them) or emerge as victims. And this is increasingly the position in which they find themselves. Liberation, equality, laws against sexual harassment, are ultimately useless in a situation in which there is no common code of courtesy or deference. A special status is only acceptable to a society in which mutual respect is required, not by law, but by common consent, and that society no longer exists here.

Everyday notion of the lady's qualities still held by ordinary people — but scorned by the chattering classes

Nevertheless it is an extraordinary fact that the idea of the 'lady' and the 'gentleman' still engage the imagination and the memory of so many people. You will often hear people say 'He was a real gentleman' or 'Now she was what I call a lady' — used of someone of any rank or status or of none, who has attracted affectionate respect from others. The gentry and the aristocracy still use the terms, though usually in a negative sense. 'Very nice, but it must be said she wasn't quite a lady' or 'He was good company you know, but he wasn't a gentleman' — both these latter examples suggesting a coterie concept, still very much alive, of an elite who recognize each other's definitions at once.

It is the ordinary man's or woman's usage that most interests me. There is, clearly, still a sense of courtesy and the words used for it are recognized and used by ordinary men and women. It isn't used by the consensus-dominated middle classes, the 'chattering classes' as they're called, because to them the whole concept of courtesy and deference is elitist and out-dated, and bears no relation to present-day society as they see it. But it *does*, and it still means something to those who know how the outside world thinks and feels. I believe that the manners of a lady — especially the idea of the lady — persists in an obstinate refusal on the part of most people to accept a wholly anarchic and brutal world, and I think there are more of these than make up members of the 'Polite Society', but many who would welcome a return to some acceptable code of conduct which would indicate the instinct that still survives of respect and deference and affection.

It is there, though it has been stifled a good deal by the wretched performance of the Churches, with their instinct to follow the fashionable trends of society, and their reluctance to consider priests as little more than counsellors and social workers. Some more spiritual lead from this quarter would certainly help the idea of courtesy (once one of the great virtues celebrated by Spenser and so many later poets) to return to our community. It is still needed, and still present in the hearts and minds of many people, who are looking for a lead and a confirmation of their belief in the ideal of manners — of conduct, of ladies or gentlemen. An idea which is, in spite of everything, still alive, but in need of nurture and encouragement.

3

Speaking Properly

The Need for a Shared Vocabulary

George Martin

Manners and writing can both be seen as mere adherence to form

We can talk about manners and writing in several ways. One aspect, for example, of the relationship between writing and manners — or more generally, the relationship between language usage and grammar, albeit in speech or writing, and manners — is obvious enough for George Bernard Shaw to have recognized it and to have written the play *Pygmalion* about it. In that play, from Professor Higgins' careful instructions in 'proper' grammar, usage, and pronunciation, the cockney flower girl, Eliza Doolittle, learns the social code and becomes a 'proper lady', capable of participating in the highest levels of English society.

The satire is plain enough: 'Society' is a sham. It exists as a consequence of peoples' acceptance of those conventions of behaviour we call *manners*, of which approved forms of language usage and pronunciation are significant parts. With adequate training, one can overcome the ignorance of those forms of behaviour that assign one his class, and regardless of character or breeding become a member of the upper class.

Witty and perceptive as Shaw's comedy is, I do not think it explains or respects finally the role manners play in society. That is why a poem like Robert Frost's poem 'Mending Wall' strikes me as having a profounder insight into manners than does Shaw's witty play.

In the poem, it will be recalled, the speaker (Frost, we might assume) observes that 'There is something that doesn't love a wall'; hence it is that he and his neighbour must meet in the spring to rebuild the stone wall between their farms, to repair gaps that the winter freeze has left.

For Frost, the barrier is an artificial one, erected in defiance of nature and logic, and he wonders why they keep it between them, for neither of them has livestock that threatens the other. (Something in him, it would seem, doesn't love a wall.) His neighbour knows why: 'Good fences make good neighbours'. It is a piece of wisdom that he learned from his father, and he won't go behind it. He will not wonder, as Frost would have him do, what he is walling out or what he is walling in. 'Good fences make good neighbours': the expression satisfies him in a way that the Rousseau in Frost cannot comprehend.

Frost conscious of artificiality of form, but realizes it demonstrates important truths

Frost as author of the poem, of course, invites us as readers of the poem to pay deeper attention to the neighbour's words than Frost as the speaker of the poem does. The neighbour knows from memory what Frost does not, that good fences *make* good neighbours. They define what is mine from what is yours, and when we meet to maintain the wall, we become *good neighbours* who meet as neighbours meet, respecting and protecting what belongs to each other, which is the very essence of neighbourliness. To do otherwise is to revert back to nature, where neighbourliness gives way to conquest and domination of one kind or another. 'Good fences make good neighbours' is not merely an adage; it is one of the conventions of successful social life, and as such it must be respected and obeyed not as a product of reason but as an expression of the wisdom of inherited experience. It is true not because reasonable consideration of the immediate world says it is true, but because the common experience of a people — the culture — has found it to be useful. By his very questioning of the existence of the wall, Frost is intruding upon his neighbour's space, attempting to dominate his thoughts by the logical superiority of his own, and in recalling his father's phrase, 'Good fences make good neighbours', the neighbour is shoving Frost back on his side of the line and maintaining his independence.

Manners, in constructing artificial restraints, check brutal animality of unfettered nature

Manners are, of course, 'mending walls', sometimes seemingly irrational behaviours through which we make neighbourliness — society — possible. At their best, manners are those behaviours in which we respect the feelings, dignity, and privacy of others. They create the space in which we interact without offending or dominating others, a place where we can meet on a plain of equality.

Literature, inasmuch as it involves interactions of human beings, necessarily embodies manners as a part of its theme. Homer's *Odyssey* has a very definite manners component: *hospitality* — probably the most universal assertion of manners. Penelope's suitors are violators of hospitality; in his reception of the disguised Athena, Telemachus is a model host, as are Menelaus and Helen in their reception of him and as are the Phaeacians in their reception of Odysseus; and Odysseus' homecoming — his reception by the swineherd and then his treatment while in disguise at home — is presented in terms of hospitality. This hospitality has its basis in two things, reverence for the gods (who may appear as a stranger) and sympathy for the wanderer.

Civilization, as represented in Homer, depends upon mutual needs and understanding, fostered by manners

The ideal of civilization that Homer presents rests in large measure on this set of manners, a model which is embodied ironically in the Cyclops episode, where Odysseus meets the one-eyed monster who 'did not consort/ With others, but stayed apart and had a lawless mind', of a people who

> Have neither assemblies for holding council nor laws,
> But they inhabit the crests of lofty mountains,
> In hollow caves, and each dispenses the laws
> For his children and his wives and is not concerned for others.

Such people, Odysseus learns, will not give 'a guest gift…as is the custom among guest friends', for they do not fear Zeus 'the protector of supplicants and guest friends'. To the extent that they are not hospitable they exclude themselves from the human community and the civilizing effect of manners.

Even in a work so severe and in some ways primitive as *The Iliad* is, manners have a distinct place. Homer is careful to define how Achilles receives Odysseus' party when they call upon him to ask him to rejoin the war with the Trojans. Achilles says to the visiting Odysseus and Ajax,

> Peace! My two great friends. I greet your coming.
> How I have needed it! Even in my anger,

of all Akhaians, you are closest to me,

and he has his friend Patroklus prepare food and drink to honour them. Plainly, Achilles, who has alienated himself from the Greek camp, still feels strongly the need for friendship, and despite his anger he can be a gracious host to those he counts his dearest friends. These visitors — particularly Odysseus and Ajax — are, as is Achilles, dangerous men whose temperaments require the conventions of hospitality that someone like the Cyclops ignores.

Even more revealing about the function of manners among so warlike a people, is the magnificent scene in which Achilles receives Priam, who has come to ask for the body of his son Hector. There is probably no more poignant moment in literature. In his grief and rage at the death of Patroklus, Achilles has lost all human sympathy and reverence for the will of the gods, so much so that Apollo complains of him:

a man who shows no decency, implacable,
barbarous in his ways as a wild lion
whose power and intrepid heart
sway him to raid the flocks of men for meat.
That man has lost all mercy;
he has no shame — that gift that hinders mortals
but helps them, too.

On the other side is Priam, who must come to Achilles as a supplicant who throws his arms around his worst enemy's knees and appeals for hospitality:

Akhilleus
be reverent before the great gods, and take
pity on me, remember your own father.
Think of me more pitiful by far, since I
have brought myself to do what no man else
has done before — to lift to my lips the hand
of one who has killed my son.

In effect, he forces Achilles to receive him as a guest, to be reverent before the gods and to be hospitable to him as to one who has suffered as Achilles' father must suffer. What happens, of course is that these two worst enemies are united in a common grief that not only leads

Achilles to give Priam the body of his son but that also restores Achilles to humanity:

> Now in Akhilleus
> the evocation of his fathers stirred
> new longing, and an ache of grief. He lifted the
> old man's hand and gently put him by.
> Then both were overborne as they remembered:
> the old king huddled at Akhilleus' feet
> wept, and wept for Hector, killer of men,
> while great Akhilleus for his own father
> as for Patroklus once again; and sobbing
> filled the room.

But again, as in the reception of Odysseus, these are still very dangerous men whose passions must be directed and restrained under the rules of hospitality. When Priam asks to be given Hector's body immediately and be sent on his way, Achilles reveals how slender a hold his hospitality has on anger:

> Therefore, *let me be.*
> Sting my sore heart again, and even here,
> under my own roof, suppliant though you are,
> I may not spare you, sir, but trample on the
> expressed commands of Zeus.

Society and community cannot be created by mere political institutions as Plato and Aristotle believed

The Greek idea of hospitality as one of the bases of society is profound enough to be included in Dante's *Divine Comedy*, where treachery toward guests is counted among the lowest of evils in the final circle of Hell. But manners for the most part are not a major part of ancient literature. It is politics and the *polis*, not manners and society, that interest Plato and Aristotle, who had, in fact, no conception of society as we have come to know it. For Aristotle it was in the *polis* that men met on a plain of equality and freedom, where they found and exercised what is distinctive in their humanity. There rhetorical skills, not manners, defined participation in public life, and we do not get any recognition of a need for any higher order of discourse, such as that we see in the meeting between Achilles and Priam. One might argue, of course, that the rules of rhetoric are themselves forms of manners in discourse through which the rhetor attempts to move his audience to an understanding of and a desire for the good. One can point to literary works, like Swift's *Modest Proposal*, where classical rhetoric provides the 'manners of the piece', or the relationship between author an audience. And someone like Wayne Boothe can write about the 'rhetoric of fiction'. But if we are to understand the role of manners in later literature, we must begin with another conception of hospitality: Christ's teachings in St Matthew 26:34-40:

> Come, ye blessed
> of my Father, inherit the
> kingdom prepared for you from the
> foundation of the world:
> For I was an hungred and ye
> gave me meat: I was thirsty, and ye
> gave me drink: I was a stranger, and
> ye took me in:
> Naked, and ye clothed me: I was sick,
> and ye visited me: I was in
> prison, and ye came unto me…
> Inasmuch as ye have do it
> unto the least of these my
> brethren, ye have done it unto me.

Christian charity combined with chivalric notions of courtesy to include humility as well as observance of form

This teaching has, of course, far greater implications for the meaning of manners than does the Homeric code of hospitality. It speaks of man as a spiritual as well as a social being and connects social conduct with the salvation of the soul. The poor, the stranger, the prisoner, the hungry — these become the guests who are the brethren of the Lord, and in treating them well one treats the Lord well. This ideal of charity, insofar as manners are concerned, is expressed in the medieval codes of chivalry, which, linked with courtly love, provide the bases of the medieval romances and such later courtesy works as Castiglioni's *Book of the Courtier*, Spenser's *Faerie Queene*, and Sydney's *Arcadia*. In this literary tradition, manners — courtesy — become the development of the spiritual as well as the social self. Through this cultivation of the self one becomes a gentleman worthy of the lady's favours — Sir Lancelot — or one worthy to find the Holy Grail — Sir Galahad.

Sir Gawain and the Green Knight, the profoundest of the English romances, is primarily a poem of manners. The pentangle of his shield symbolises the virtues of its hero, Sir Gawain.

> The fifth of the five fives followed by this knight
> Were beneficence boundless and brotherly love
> And pure mind and manners, that none might impeach,
> And compassion most precious — these peerless five
> Were forged and made fast in him, foremost of men.

The Virgin Mary is 'his lady', 'on the inner part of his shield her image portrayed'. His quest is for the Green Knight, to whom he owes a blow with an axe as the completion of the Christmas game they have played in which they vow to swap blows. It is in terms of hospitality, however, that his manners and his character are tested. On Christmas Eve, alone in the wild, in answer to his prayer to his Lady, he sees 'a castle as comely as a knight could own', and he offers thanks 'To Jesus and Saint Julian [the patron saint of hospitality] that are gentle both/ That had in courteous accord inclined to his prayers'. There he meets with a host who is the soul of hospitality — 'the lord himself descends from his chamber/ To meet with good manners the man on his floor'. Of Sir Gawain the household says:

> Now displays of deportment shall dazzle our eyes
> And the polished pearls of impeccable speech;
> The high art of eloquence is ours to pursue
> Since the father of fine manners is found in our midst.
> Great is God's grace, and goodly indeed,
> That a guest such as Gawain he guides to us here
> When men sit and sing of the Saviour's birth in view.
> With command of manners pure
> He shall each hurt imbue;
> Who shares his converse, sure,
> Shall learn love's language true.

But there is another trial set for him, another Christmas game to be played that tries his character as well as his manners. The lord of the house provides the terms of the game:

Whatever I win in the wood shall be yours
And chance you shall meet shall be mine in exchange.

The lady of the house, who for three mornings comes to his room plainly offering him her favours. His test is to resist her offers (out of loyalty to Mary and out of respect for his host) without offending her, while remaining true to his pledge to his host to exchange each day's takings. For the host, each day it is the prey from that day's hunt; for Sir Gawain, it is the kisses he has received from the lady and her charmed garter, which he prudently withholds. The trial becomes a lesson in which Sir Gawain learns that true humility is not just mannerly conduct. It is grounded in and proceeds from a knowledge of human frailty, the knowledge that Sir Gawain obtains and brings back to King Arthur's court to be the basis for a new Order of the Garter.

Chivalrous conduct, as developed by latter writers, evolved into regard for good form in speech and behaviour as a sign of good character

It would be hard, on the evidence of the literature of the Renaissance, to overstate how deeply this chivalry penetrated the ideal of courtly conduct. It gave rise to such plays as Shakespeare's *Love's Labours Lost* and *Twelfth Night*, and was the basis of numerous court masques. Most important, however, was its influence on, and place within, the novels and plays of the emerging upper middle-class of the eighteenth and nineteenth centuries. Comedies of Manners and Novels of Manners create a social environment in which rural and middle classes play out their lives as if they were members of court, using the manners derived from courtly love and chivalry as standards of social conduct. *She Stoops to Conquer*, *Pride and Prejudice*, even Pope's wonderful *Rape of the Lock*, derive their significance from the ideal of manners they assume. At their best, these manners are refinements of human behaviour that reflect a developed sensibility, grounded in ideals of good conduct. Good manners are associated with good character, so that in a novella by Henry James, such as *The Pupil*, a breach in etiquette — dressing in the drawing room — signals a breakdown in character. In such a society eloquence of speech or writing is an acquired skill, reflective of social values. To speak well, to write well, these are social accomplishments, a part of the manners of a well-defined society, part of the refinement of one's character.

The grammar of manners the foundation for the moral vocabulary which allows members of society to communicate

Society is not the sham Shaw thinks it is, nor are manners the absurd conservatism Frost's spokesman thinks they are. They are the grammar of social life, conventions of behaviour which define the level of civilization a people or a person has obtained. The learning of manners has ever been a part of one's social development, and the development of manners is an indication of how developed a people's social life has become, ie, the kinds of social interactions they have made possible.

These manners are the 'grammar' of society, its rules of usage, which bring society into existence in the same way that grammars make sense out of noise. On a basic level, these manners are as natural to social order as driving on one's own side of the highway is to motor travel, for they are created out of social necessities for the meanest kind of social existence. To ignore them borders on and frequently is included in conceptions of criminal behaviour.

Lack of a moral vocabulary and behavioural grammar inevitably precludes social dialogue

Novels and comedies of manners persist, but they persist mostly as satires, as in the recent television comedy *Keeping up Appearances*. American literature, particularly Mark Twain's *Tom Sawyer* and *Huckleberry Finn* made an end to manners as the meaningful thematic context of literature. What matters to Holdin Caldfield, the 'catcher in the rye', is being what Huck wants to be — just himself. 'I gotta be me', becomes the universal theme. Dramatic dialogue, the kind of witty engagement we find in a play like *The Importance of Being Ernest* or *A Woman of No Consequence*, seems to be out of the reach of dramatists who depend upon frequency of obscenities for humour. Saul Bellow's Mr Samler has it right when he wonders about a society that makes excrement the fundamental standard of value judgement.

4

Knowing Your Place

Manners Between the Generations

Anthony O'Hear

Manners in the 1950's: deference as a means of marking appropriate differences

As a boy, I was taught to give my seat up to an old person on a bus or train. When a grown-up came into a room, I had to stand up, and speak politely if, but only if they spoke to me. One raised one's cap to an adult or a teacher one met in the street. We did not, of course, have television or computer games, but had there been such things, they would certainly have been turned off if older people entered the room.

Sometimes, it is true, one endured what seemed like hours of boredom, listening to conversations in which one could not participate. In retrospect, though, the orderly exclusion from adult exchange was important. It taught that there were states of being to which one might one day aspire, however remarkable it might have seemed at the time. There was also the sense, immensely comforting at the time, that one day one might enjoy the settled, confident outlook on life which adults had as a matter of course. And when an adult turned to talk to one, as the well-mannered ones did from time to time, they made it clear that they were behaving in a way different from their norm. But this, too, was consoling. They recognized the difference between themselves and you, and in so doing, picked you out as distinctive, as an individual occupying a particular station in life, and not as some cipher indistinguishable from any other person, young or old. We thus begun to learn that individuality flourishes against a background of settled expectations, within which true and deep differences between people can emerge and develop. Manners were the external sign that one behaved differently according to the different stations one had reached in one's journey through life, and according to the station of one's interlocutor. And all this was a source of harmless pride, as well, the sixth-former no longer rapped over the knuckles for having his hands in his pockets or no cap on his head, and — up to a point — talking to masters on a level resembling adult discourse. It was a source of pride, because all this was, in a curious way, earned. One had been through all kinds of experiences, painful and pleasant, but necessarily endured, in order to take on the manners of a different station.

Appropriate behaviour fosters impression of appropriate status

I do not know whether at the deepest level, that of which Kierkegaard and the existentialists speak, that at which the individual stands naked before his Maker or the reality of death or whatever is one's ultimate fate, adults of my youth were much more in control of their lives than are the adults of today. One of our teachers gassed himself in a bed-sitter in Finsbury Park, for what reason we never knew. But at the less deep but no less significant level of everyday existence, adults certainly were more in control. They were more in control, because they acted with more control. In their dress and behaviour they carried themselves with a measure of dignity rarely seen today. By carrying themselves outwardly with dignity, they became dignified within, certainly to the extent that they knew the measure of things and the responses appropriate to different circumstances. Perhaps even at the deepest level, my poor geography teacher notwithstanding, the idea that there is a right way of behaving according to one's age and position, and the experience which comes with behaving in the right way, may intimate that in the universe, too, there is a measure of things, and so alleviate the angst Kierkegaard and his followers would wish on us all.

Continual adjustment of behaviour required throughout life with manners providing the model for each age's correct demeanour

Life is indubitably a journey from birth to death. It is also a journey with different stages and landmarks. Different types of behaviour are appropriate and natural at different stages of life: an enthusiastic enquiring volubility and experimentation when young, a controlled strength and display and pride when first in adulthood, an easy, masterful superiority when fully mature, developing, when older, into a calm, dignified appropriation of wisdom and experience, and finally a sense manifested in how one does what one does that this world is, as indeed it is, transient. To the excesses and faults intrinsic to each of these stages, civilized manners apply an acceptable surface. So the very young have to learn to curb their impetuosity and, as pupils and students to defer to the knowledge and experience of their elders. Adolescents and young adults have to confine their desires and their strength through courtesy and the rituals of courtship. Those in first middle age must soften their aggressiveness and sense of superiority through a modest demeanour and acceptance of such social duties as politeness to acquaintances, even if inferior, and the giving of hospitality and time, to those who have a claim on one, even to bores. And the elderly have to avoid the bitterness and cynicism which experience can bring through a cultivation of gentleness in their behaviour and a renewed interest in the young, often via love of grandchildren.

Continual inculcation of manners permits spontaneity which should characterize them

Traditionally, the manners appropriate to each stage of life have been encoded in the customs of the society to which one belongs. Education has had it as an important part of its role to inculcate these customs in the young, so that in due time they become second nature. As manners are supposed to be second nature and can fulfil their role only when acted on instantly and unthinkingly, a society which has to produce books on etiquette is either already lost to the barbarism of impulse, or is one in which what should be an adjunct to life and to the life of a society has become an end in itself.

While there may have been eras in which the latter was the case — eighteenth century France, perhaps — our situation is one in which the barbarism of impulse reigns. Self-styled counsellors and psychotherapists advise their 'clients' (who are clients precisely because they are getting the advice they want) that feelings should never be suppressed, but always expressed and usually, I imagine, acted upon. On the contrary, first feelings should usually be suppressed, rarely acted upon, and always clad in the forms of manners. Otherwise all we will have is what in fact we have all too often: a society of individuals who have lost all hope of individuality in becoming no more than slaves to their (naturally inarticulate) passions and cries of anger or lust or pleasure or whatever primitive feeling they have. At that level, we are all the same; not so much the skull beneath the skin as the flesh beneath the garments which distinguish the socialized human being from the a-social animal.

The notion of 'authenticity' and doctrine of bad faith as destructive of manners

The young are, of course, easily attracted to the thought that naked feelings and naked bodies are somehow more authentically human than the manners which disguise feeling and the clothes which cover our nakedness. They forget that clothes and institutions and social structures, and the manners which go with these things are actually the very things which make us human, authentically so, and against which significant differences between us can develop and be revealed. These, though, are truths which tend to become appreciated only with experience. The young thus find highly seductive the notion of Sartrean bad faith.

In his famous existentialist treatise, *Being and Nothingness*, Sartre writes of the waiter in the café:

> His movement is quick and forward a little too precise, a little too rapid. He comes toward the patrons with a step a little too quick. He bends forward a little too eagerly; his voice, his eyes express an interest a little too solicitous for the order of the customer. Finally then he returns trying to imitate in his walk the flexible stiffness of some kind of automaton while carrying his tray with the recklessness of a tight-rope walker by putting it in a perpetually unstable, perpetually broken equilibrium which he perpetually re-establishes by a light movement of the arm and hand. All his behaviour seems to us a game. (p 59)

It is this seeming a game to which we are supposed to object. In truth, there is something in what Sartre says. Formal manners, particularly those of someone like a waiter, do have something of play-acting about them, especially before they become second nature when, without ceasing to be artifice, they cease to be artificial.

'Authenticity' prohibits the individual from adapting to structures of society and restricts his ability to act

While Sartre, and other prophets of authenticity may object, there are many occasions in life where we know that it is better to mask our initial, usually hostile or selfish feelings. Concern for the other demands no less, as does one's own interest in living in a peaceful and orderly society, one not dominated by the aggressiveness or surliness of the stronger-willed. Anyone who had the misfortune to be 'served' by an Aeroflot hostess in communist days will need no convincing that even an over-unctuous, self-conscious, play-acting waiter is preferable to one with no manners at all. Nor, in any case, is it true that there is no mid-point between the camp figure Sartre describes and the thuggish harridans who occupied good jobs in the USSR.

Egalitarianism and bad manners: failure to recognize status leads to random self-satisfaction

The destruction of manners in the USSR had been deliberate policy, not so much in anticipation of Sartre's doctrine of bad faith, as a part of an attempt to destroy the old social order. The way in which manners do, as we have already seen, mark differences in achievement and status, is also something the young often find irksome, attracted as they are to notions of egalitarian democracy in which all such differences are disguised and discounted.

The connection between radical democracy and unmannerliness was noticed long ago by Plato in *The Republic* (561 ff). In such a society, impulse is king. Insolence is called 'good breeding', licence 'liberty', prodigality 'magnificence' and shamelessness 'manly spirit'. Day by day, citizens indulge the appetite of the day, first winebibbing, then abandoning themselves to lascivious music, then drinking only water and dieting, then exercising, then neglecting exercise, then doing philosophy, then going in for politics, and bouncing up and saying whatever comes into their heads, then turning to military activity, and then to money-making. Manners, of course, would put a break on such impetuosity, partly because of the way they surround the activities in question with ritual and order, and partly because of the way they suggest that most of them require serious training and initiation before they can be engaged in. The arbitrary and unmannerly picking-up and putting down of activities is characteristic of market-oriented societies, such as that envisaged by *The Sunday Times*, in which consumer choice reigns, untrammelled by tradition, authority or, indeed, manners.

If the doctrine of bad faith and egalitarian democracy (whether of a communist or a consumerist stripe) are naturally attractive to the young, and also naturally destructive of civilized manners, it is arguable that good manners in our society have been undermined far more by the middle-aged and the old than by the young. After all, unmannerliness and hostility to good breeding among the young are to be expected, and are no new thing. Manners can survive that, if society as a whole holds firm, and, the elders — those in charge — uphold standards.

Behaviour of ageing trendies undermines possibility of moral and well-mannered future generations

But this means, first and foremost, that they act their age, and it is this which many of our current leaders — children of the 1960s, the age of eternal youth, remember — steadfastly refuse to do. We have Vice-Chancellors with earrings, aristocrats as hippies and public relations 'consultants' criticising the Prince of Wales for one of his few accomplishments, his sober sense of dress; the leaders of our political parties are in their 40s or early 50s and we are surprised that they lack gravitas or authority; presidents jog in public in the most appalling plastic garments, as if they were actors or popstars; bishops use their first names on television and Radio One. We are in a society in which no one wishes to appear old or act their age. It is not so much the young, who after all have nothing to forget, as the old who have forgotten their manners; and if they forget, who will teach the young?

Plato had foreseen this, too. In the anarchic state in which the old disguise their age

> the father habitually tries to resemble the child and is afraid of his sons, and the son likens himself to the father and feels no awe or fear of his parents, so that he may be forsooth a free man...The teacher in such a case fears and fawns upon the pupils, and the pupils pay no heed to the teacher...In general the young ape their elders and vie with them in speech and action, while the old, accommodating themselves to the young, are full of pleasantry and graciousness, imitating the young for fear of appearing sour or despotic. (*Republic*, 563)

In my youth, the trendy vicar on his motor-bike, or the teacher talking about Elvis Presley or Cliff Richard were figures of fun, universally derided for not acting in accordance with their age or status. Nowadays, the Dean and Chapter of Winchester Cathedral, organise a 'rave in the nave' of their magnificent and holy building; headmasters put on sweat-bands and T-shirts, as if they were superannuated tennis players, and strum guitars in school performances of musicals. The Very Rev Trevor Beeson, Dean of Winchester justified the introduction of Cross Reference, Azimuth Brain-storm and Fresh Claim into William of Wykeham's great cathedral on the grounds that 'the main thing is that the young people have a good time'.

The main thing is certainly not that young people have a good time, and even if it were, it is certainly not for the hierarchy to say so. The condescension involved is, in any case, manifest. Does Rev Beeson listen to pop music by choice, or, in the secrecy of the Cathedral Close, does he surreptitiously listen to Henry Purcell and Palestrina? It is difficult to decide which is worse: a (presumably) middle-aged clergyman who actually likes pop music or one who, while not liking it, desecrates his cathedral by having it so that the young people should have a good time. Instinctively, everyone, including the young, feels there is something wrong in all of this: and what is wrong is the lack of manners involved in the old failing to act their age.

Acting one's age: better a young fogey than an ageing trendy

Life is, as I have said, a journey. Different types of behaviour are appropriate to the different ages. This sense of what is appropriate is encoded in manners regarding dress and behaviour. A 16 year-old with a pince-nez and pin-striped suit who does nothing but read metaphysical poetry and attend Mass at Brompton Oratory may be a young fogey. We would like to see him, occasionally at least, out with a girl or on the rugby field or on a camping holiday — where there are also important truths to be learned and important consolations to be had. But far more foolish, and far more dangerous to society as a whole, is it when the middle-aged — who, after all, should have the experience and wisdom to know better — comport themselves as if they were young: when they dye their hair, have their faces lifted and wear baseball caps back to front (or even the right way round) and shell suits and trainers; when they buy exercise bicycles, jog in public and go ten-pin bowling and listen to pop on walkmans; when they go to wine bars and discos with their secretaries; when they talk to the young as if they, too, were young.

Excess of manners leads at worst to excess formality: lack of manners leads to a denial of mortality

A society in which age does not act its age is far sicker than one which suffers from the occasional exaggerated waiter or even a surfeit of manners. A lack of suitable manners in the aged is nothing less than a refusal to admit their own mortality, and a society in which the fact of mortality is systematically occluded is one that has forgotten its sense of proportion. Of such a society, Eliot's plea strikes home:

Do not let me hear
Of the wisdom of old men, but rather of their folly,
The fear of fear and frenzy, their fear of possession,
Of belonging to another, or to others, or to God.
The only wisdom we can hope to acquire
Is the wisdom of humility: humility is endless.

A lack of the manners appropriate to one's age or status is above all a lack of humility. And in the case of the old, a lack of such humility is particularly painful, because instead of the dignity we found in the elderly of our youth, we find only the frenzy of those who do not want to admit their age. Despite, or perhaps because of their comparatively greater wealth and all the state benefits they are accorded, the middle-aged and old of today conspicuously lack the quiet dignity and sombre manners of those who were old in my youth.

Small wonder the young are bad-mannered if the old do not act their age. A revival of manners can begin only when the old discard the garments and habits of youth, and begin once more to acknowledge their age and their mortality.

5

Keeping up Appearances

Clothes as a Public Matter

Athena S Leoussi

Clothes an outward sign of personality and age of wearer

In his famous essay, *The Heroism of Modern Life* of 1846, Charles Baudelaire accounted for the dark clothing of the men of Paris as 'the outer husk of the modern hero' and as possessing a 'political beauty, which is an expression of the public soul'. This was because 'all centuries and peoples have their own form of beauty [and] so inevitably we have ours'.[1] Baudelaire's observations are of dual significance to an analysis of our contemporary manners of dress. First, he contends that the black varnished boots, coat and top hat of his contemporaries somehow projected the political experiences and ideals of France at that time; that dress is a document of cultural expression. Secondly, his evaluation of that particular form of dress as being just one among the infinitely varied forms which beauty can take, documents the anti-Enlightenment Romanticism which, since the late eighteenth century, has been, with its rival, a cultural imperative in the Western world.

To claim now after Baudelaire and, indeed, after James Laver's classic study, *Taste and Fashion from the French Revolution to the Present Day*,[2] that dress is expressive, that the costume of the period is the mirror of the soul, of the *Zeitgeist*, might be so trivial as to seem impertinent. But, on the one hand, the chaotic excesses to which the liberal élite has been driven by the logic of freedom, and, on the other, an understanding of the actual significance of this statement, justify a discussion of modern dress in its relevance to the demands of the inner life of human beings.

The political and cultural pluralism which we experience daily in the different spheres of our social life, in our eating habits and entertainment, in literature, art, political parties, old and new religions, education, and so on, makes the use of the term *Zeitgeist* too narrow a hypothesis for the apprehension of the cultural significance of the modern manners of dress. In the context of the present farrago of styles of dress, I propose to look critically at certain tendencies which seem to me to go against the very ideas of both culture and of cultural pluralism.[3] If it is true that the manner in which we clothe our bodies and present them daily to ourselves and to the outside world serves not only utilitarian purposes, but also projects and even realizes the moral, aesthetic and conceptual aspirations of ourselves and of that world, then in certain forms of contemporary dress, all these multiple and indeed simultaneous uses of dress are overlooked in indifference, selectively pursued or rejected outright.

Utilitarian dress: rejecting aesthetic appeal for the practicality of jeans

One of the most disturbing tendencies in modern dress manners is the supposed utilitarian or instrumental attitude to dress. This attitude has led to the introduction into modern everyday dress manners of a new type of clothing, the denim trousers. This attitude to dress is not only just sub-cultural, but anti-cultural. In fact, the utilitarian attitude to dress has led to the cultural impoverishment of everyday life. Mere utility in matters of dress means the rejection of the aesthetic and communicative power of clothing, of colour, texture and cut, its power to embody and communicate ideas of value. As Roger Scruton has observed, the sartorial imperative goes beyond the physical protection of the body from the elements, the keeping of the body warm or cool or dry and at the same time flexible.[4] People do not and indeed have not made, bought and worn clothes for this reason alone, the reason of utility. Men do not design clothes with just their meteorological or, indeed, their mechanical appropriateness in mind, that is, their suitability for the various movements of the body when it is engaged in this or that particular physical task.

Indeed, even the choice to wear jeans in modern city-life is more often than not determined by non-utilitarian reasons. Jeans are chosen for their *expressiveness*, not their utility. They belong to the sphere of religion, not the economy. Jeans are for cowboys, ie, for strenuous physical work. They are not for shop or desk work which are the activities with which most of their wearers daily busy themselves. Tight jeans are even less utilitarian even for normal physiological activities such as breathing, walking and sitting. To wear jeans indiscriminately, without regard for the social situation, is to take a stand. Jeans herald not an occupation but a particular conception of interpersonal behaviour. This behaviour is symbolically, albeit naively, promised to be matter-of-fact and for this reason preferable to any other. But what this promise really means is the behaviour towards an animal in the corral or a drain pipe; not a human being. Men and women in jeans offer other men and women the violent, cold and limited life of dire necessity, not humanity.

Gym clothing worn when not exercising indicates healthist neuroses

The expansion of utilitarian forms of dress beyond the circumstances for which they were designed has introduced new manners of dress and with them new mores in the social situations into which they were exported. Take, for example, keep-fit gear and particularly the leggings and the track-suit with its adjuncts, the trainers and the sweat-shirt. We no longer find these forms of clothing in the gym or the rehearsal room of a theatre for which they were conceived, but in bank queues, on the street, in the supermarket, the classroom, the office, the art gallery, the party, the home. Such usages are not applications of these minimalist, clinging, uncluttered, muscle-warming, durable and malleable garments to new uses, but rather moral innovations and, indeed, transgressions.

The modern obsession with physical health and its pursuit through physical exercise has absorbed the varied activities and interests of modern men and women into one alone, if not in substance, at least in appearance. It has thus reduced all the different sites of contemporary life into the different sectors of a gymnasium. Men queue for buses in track-suits as if in preparation for the decathlon. The cultural consequence of the modern *cultus* of physical fitness, of life in service of the body, is, as in Thomas and Matthew Arnold's time, a reduction of the spiritual life of the individual, a loss of cultural balance. This one-sided physical culture is also detrimental to civility, to the social considerations which any human behaviour, including the introduction of one's physical self to the presence of others, involves. At the very least, the utilitarian manner of dress denies the fact that one's appearance has an aesthetic dimension and, indeed, an aesthetic effect on others, and thus rejects one's aesthetic obligations to others. It bears no decoration. It is not meant to please but to function like a piece of mechanical equipment. To wear a track-suit in public outside the gym means to ignore this public.

The dress of Pan: the rejection of beauty from clothing

The disdain for the aesthetic appeal of one's physical appearance is observable everywhere, but mostly among the young. The religion of utility is only a partial explanation. A more complete explanation can be found in the Romanticism of the so-called post-modern condition of Western man. As Bernice Martin has observed in her magnificent work, *A Sociology of Contemporary Cultural Change*, the Expressive Revolution of the 1960s ushered into Western culture a new era of romantic manners and morals.[5]

In manners of dress as in all other matters, romanticism meant pantheism. The belief that 'everything goes' was anti-structural; it set out to dissolve all the inherited distinctions and boundaries of the social order. In the aesthetics of dress this belief dissolved the distinction between the beautiful and the ugly. It claimed that everything was beautiful. The result was the glorification of ugliness.

Costume creates society and shared aesthetic sensibility

Dress is a device of beauty. Dress gives ordinary men and women the opportunity to improve themselves and to enrich the quality of their everyday lives by pursuing daily a world and a self fairer than they found it. Dress allows men and women to control, through their appearance, the impressions which they give both to themselves and to others. Dress can cover blemishes and imperfections in our bodies and enhance those forms and colorations which satisfy our particular, time-bound conception of human physical beauty. In fact, any conception of human beauty will do. One should never been seen without one, and this for no other reason than the respect for ourselves and for our fellows. Indeed, we may say, following the great Victorian humanist-*cum*-aesthete Walter Pater,

> Given the hardest terms, supposing our days are indeed but a shadow, even so, we may well adorn and beautify, in scrupulous self-respect, our souls, and whatever our souls touch upon — these wonderful bodies, these material dwelling places through which the shadows pass together for a while, the very raiment we wear...[6]

Finally, a pleasant appearance creates positive impressions and, by attracting men and women to one another, it creates society.

Abandoning a sense of aesthetic appeal in favour of shapeless slovenliness

To believe that every body is beautiful is to force men to be, or to pretend to be, indifferent to form. But the repression of the aesthetic impulse in matters of human physical appearance can only be done at one's own peril. Such repression causes dress to lose its aesthetic meaning and men the power to turn ugly ducklings into swans, to transform raw nature into culture: to turn the human body into a work of art, a pleasure to the eye. To abandon one's reliance on dress is to dispense with our body, first as a site of everyday cultural creation and secondly as an instrument of influence.

Romantic aesthetics have found expression in a number of new manners of dress but especially in the calculated neglect of one's appearance. 'Why don't people care any more [about their appearance], why do they turn up for work with pierced noses, odd socks, no socks or smelly feet?' Christa D'Souza enquires.[7] Although one may not agree with her answer, which attributes such neglect to the poor state of the economy and its disheartening and demotivating effect on people, the neglect of one's appearance is clearly a recognized fact among social observers.

The neglectful manner of dress also involves the wearing of loose clothing. Such clothing avoids any definition of form and, in so doing, evades formal judgement. This is a romantic strategy. The wearing of leggings out of doors as part of normal everyday dress and regardless of the forms which they contain, also belongs to this style. The wearing of leggings, whether one has the figure or not, but especially when one has not, is part of the romantic aesthetics of the equal value of all forms. The wearers of leggings deny the idealization of the human form which they display with the crudeness and arrogance which all levelling, ie, undiscriminating, ideologies encourage. How very different this is even from the classical dress of Greek antiquity whose aim too was the affirmation of the human form. As Anne Hollander has observed, 'classical drapery…also exists to reveal the body', but to the *advantage* of the body. To this end it selects, conceals and reveals, caresses its contours, intelligently, subtly and humbly. How very different this affirmation of the body is from the modern flaunting of legs of all sizes and shapes in the public face.

A desire to appear presentable not vanity but recognition of one's effect on others

To care for the comeliness of one's appearance is not a trivial pursuit. It is an intellectual and moral activity for it involves judgement, self-restraint and love. It involves the capacity to notice things, to make comparisons in matters of form, colour and social situation; it involves the disciplines of diet and physical exercise as opposed to self-indulgence; and it involves the sympathetic concern for the effect which one's appearance has on the well-being of others.

Romanticism in dress also involves the Platonic trivialization of dress as mere appearance in favour of some inward substance, a real self who dwells underneath the clothing. But this self always proves to be amorphous and in perpetual existential flux because the romantic personality is universalist and emotional. It makes no reasoned choices and hence no commitments.

Sex and violence in modern dress manners: a reflection of aggressive self-assertion

Dress is more than a device which keeps us warm in winter and cool in summer; much more. Dress is also about taboos, ie, inhibitions. And the most powerful and tabooed forces in human social life are human sexuality and violence. Over the centuries, men have seen in particular forms of clothing, so many devices for the human mastery of these primeval forces. Certain modern fashions of dress, however, endeavour to do the opposite: to allow these forces to master men.

The affirmation of sex and violence in modern manners of dress can be seen in the often virtual disappearance of dress itself from many parts of the human body to which it used to be applied, and in the popularity of clothes made of animal skins (leather) or imitating their patterns. Such 'raiment' calls men back to the jungle, to the pre-civilizational state, and turns modern cities into zoos. Fashion magazines promote the 'wild look' for both men and women and turn them into leopards, zebras and tigers.

To condemn clothing inspired by natural motifs is to show a complete lack of taste and even of understanding and this is not what I propose to do. Indeed, the tiger style could be associated with the ecological sensitivities of the day, ie, the desire to protect wild species from extinction as much as with purely decorative judgements. However, these same motifs are also part of the anti-culture of permissiveness which set out to break all taboos and which obliged men and women to express themselves without inhibition, even when there was nothing of any value for anyone to express. In fact, animal motifs in dress display the logical culmination of this so-called pluralist culture, namely the *dissolution* of all culture into barbarity. They are the motifs of the culture of militant self-assertion, infinite and arbitrary rights and zero obligations.

Leather jackets are matched with guerilla headbands, pierced noses, studded leather boots, aggressive tattoos. Such items of dress are warfare gear. They are declarations of war, the war of the sexes, the generations, the classes, the war of all against all, if not in practice, at least in mood and on the level of symbols. It is remarkable how much ingenuity is going into the transformation of civilian clothing into military uniforms. Such clothes make the end of society thinkable and cultivate suspicion. And suspicion erodes one's willingness to give and makes co-operation impossible either in the pub or at the job interview.

Certain trends in modern clothing do not only disclaim the peace treaties of civilized society, they also attack sexual taboos by asserting the sexual mores of animals. More often than not, this form of dress is only playful. Those who wear it do not really mean what they 'say'. But the fact that the sign exists and that this *is* what it can be taken to mean, does attest to a malaise with modern sexual mores.

Of course, the animal in us is a fact of human life and, indeed, a part of conscious, civilized life. Civilization does not repress human sexuality, rather it humanises it and marries it to love. Dress partakes in this civilization of human sexuality. It hides the sexual parts from the public gaze and thus withdraws individual sexuality from the public sphere. Dress makes one's sexual parts taboo, ie, unavailable to the multitude, and thereby allows one's sexuality to be one's own private matter. The privatisation of sexuality forces and, indeed, empowers the individual to choose his or her partner and to do so on more considered, personal grounds. Reason and love must come before the sexual act. Dress does not repress sexuality *per se* but, as Robert Grant has observed, its public display.[8] Dress, by setting the naked body apart makes it holy, special. And this special status of the body, its reservation for one alone, is what gives the sexual encounter a heightened, human meaning.

The revival of 1960s clothing and the vulgar display of sexuality

The sexual revolution of the 1960s rejected the inherited injunction that the sexual parts be publicly concealed. It had, and continues to have, a tremendous effect on dress manners. Indeed, our contemporary manners of clothing go back to the Expressive Revolution of the 1960s not only as a continuation of its spirit but also, and more recently, as an explicit revival of its forms: the mini-skirt, hipster and flared trousers, tight, short and ribbed jumpers. The protest element of 1960s-revival dress is evident in a revealing statement in the magazine *Clothes Show*, aimed at young girls. An article in the February 1995 issue, entitled 'The Girlfriend', recommended above the waist glitter vest, hipster trousers and a diamanté necklace. The stated aim of such clothing was to shock, to be anti-moralistic: 'If looks could kill. Shock fashion tactics to really annoy his mum…Mama…just didn't think nice girls should dress that way'.

Post-revolutionary clothing promises to liberate human sexuality from its artificial and exploitative ties. But this liberation of the sexual self means the detachment of sexuality from the love, trust, protection and intimacy of the 'bourgeois' home and a new attachment, the bondage to the impersonal, cold, cruel and fluctuating appetites of the *agora*; not the communitarian innocence and pleasures of the garden of Eden.

The sexuality of the female body is more diffused than that of the male. Consequently, the exposure of any one part of it has an erotic significance. Modern female dress manners, in keeping with modern sexual morals, is perforated and minimalist. Leggings too enter the game of undress, revealing more than concealing the lower half of the female anatomy. For this *is* a game, albeit a dangerous one, and the need for closure is maintained as nobody admits that 'the emperor (or empress) wears no clothes'. Nevertheless, there is something intensely vulgar and tactless in the declaration of the body as open to all. It is like ripping off the doors of lavatories in a *nostalgie de la boue*.

PVC dresses and trousers which cling to the body like leather, are another device for the modern affirmation of the body and its imperatives — while at the same time being animal friendly! The desire to destroy the sexual and other social orders, to create chaos, is also evident in the very names of clothes designers such as 'Chaos Creators', whose products can be obtained, significantly, from a shop called 'Sign of the Times'.

Sexuality is also related to gender roles. And dress plays a major role in gender socialization. The romantic revolution of anti-structure, of de-differentiation, produced the unisex manner of dress and accessories. Women wear trouser suits and both men and women wear

Calvin Klein's perfume 'CK One'. The danger of de-differentiation lies in its extremes. Everyone would agree that trousers fit both the professional and decorous needs of the female architect who must climb up scaffolds. But to destroy the category of gender altogether as 'socially constructed' is to go against nature, not society.

Dress not merely a private preference, but morally, socially and culturally significant

For the liberal logic which dominates the cultural and political thought of the modern Atlantic world, dress is a personal matter. I have tried to show that this is not the case and that the act of clothing our bodies involves social and, indeed, cultural considerations. Dress involves others in that it projects a particular definition of the situation, namely our plan for the way in which we intend to co-operate with those with whom we are in immediate physical proximity. Dress is significant because men have understood its power and harnessed its possibilities to their cultural choices.

Although fashion is a site of the exercise of individual freedom in liberal democratic societies, nevertheless pluralism in dress, and thereby in our attitudes to our body, can easily degenerate into anomie. It is our responsibility as citizens of such privileged societies to be vigilant over the maintenance not only of individual freedom, but also of reason and of cultural value in all spheres of human activity, and to transmit these to future generations as vital guides to human happiness.

I have also criticized the post-Freudian pastoral naivetés of modern romantic mores which seek to glorify pre-social animal man. Modern aggressive undress is not only an abandonment of taste but also of the values of understanding, fellowship and personal commitment.

I have argued against utilitarianism in modern dress, favouring a more organic understanding of the spiritual and physical sides of man. It is a quality of the human mind to turn the physical objects which enter into its remit into cultural objects: to define their structure, beauty and appropriateness to human intercourse. Our clothes are no exception.

In our modern civilized world, it is not enough to wear something warm or cool depending on the weather. Our daily morning toilette is not determined by the weather forecast alone. Since the Great Awakening of the Enlightenment, and indeed since Kant, we cannot escape the imperatives of culture, which are the imperatives of humanity, namely our intellectual, moral and aesthetic obligations to ourselves and to others. I have argued that dress is a cultural outlet. Consequently, we ought to take the ways in which we clothe our bodies and present them to ourselves and to the world seriously, that is, as a specifically cultural and social activity. Furthermore, we ought to take every day as yet another opportunity in which to realize our highest cultural aspirations. Dress enables us to invest our daily life with cultural significance.

6

Playing the Game

Sport and the Learning of Manners

Simon Green

Cricket once seen as creating 'gentlemen' but professionalism increasingly undermining civilizing ethos

The Japanese, it seems, are taking up cricket. The young, and especially the university-aged young, are learning the game with the enthusiasm of converts. But their sponsors in this noble quest are seldom, so we learn, the sports departments of their respective institutions. Typically, such support comes from the seemingly more distant faculties of sociology. Why? Because it is the accompanying, cultivated *manners* as much as the primary, physical purposes, more especially the public display of civilized — one might once have said sporting — values which supposedly accompany its performance, that really attract the modern Japanese to cricket. Specifically, it is the sense of 'fair play' and of 'being a good sport', or of knowing how to win and how to lose, and of how to do both with good grace and to the benefit of all participants, a sense and a knowledge particularly associated with the cultivation of wider, gentlemanly virtues, which the Japanese are apparently seeking from their new pastime. And there is some reason to believe that they may actually find them there.[1]

Certainly, Prime Minister Robert Mugabe of Zimbabwe, one-time terrorist supremo and erstwhile Marxist theoretician of pan-African liberation, has recently been of this view. In his own words:

> Cricket civilizes people and creates good gentlemen. I want everyone to play cricket in Zimbabwe; I want ours to be a nation of gentlemen.[2]

To be sure, political cynics might point here to a tone of universal compulsion which speaks as much of the old-time totalitarian as for the newly-discovered educator in the polite arts. Similarly, a social historian of English (and even of colonial) manners might reasonably doubt the continuing ability of the game to sustain a truly elevated ethos amongst its practitioners. We live, after all, in the era of Merv Hughes rather than of Sir Pelham Warner; or, for that matter, of Victor Trumper. Put another way, we now expect our cricketers to swear, to cheat and to lie; that is, to be professionals rather than sportsmen.[3]

But this was not once the case. In fact, it was not the case even quite a short time ago. As recently as 1961, England's international, or Test, team was captained by a man who was not only widely acknowledged to be the finest batsman of his era, described by an expert contemporary as 'a great batsman' who '[o]n his day could scatter any attack'; but also a man whose 'manners', the same authority reported, 'were a tribute both to his home and his school', one who 'lived according to his own high ethical standards' and who was 'acutely conscious of his responsibilities, and his position'.[4] His name was Peter May. The sheer range, and the very moving quality, of the tributes paid to May after his death in December 1994 suggest that he more than fulfilled those responsibilities and altogether more than justified his privileged position. In the fitting words of Christopher Martin-Jenkins,

> he was a champion and a hero [who] through his patriotism and determination...made the best of a wonderful natural talent [yet] was as genuinely humble and self-effacing as any great sportsman can ever have been.[5]

Amateurism and love of fair play did not diminish competitiveness

Peter May was a public schoolboy. He was educated at Charterhouse, there a contemporary of Lords Prior and Rees-Mogg. He was also a Cambridge graduate and university sportsman, a blue in both soccer and cricket. Later he was a batsman at Surrey and captain of England for a record 41 tests. Yet he remained an amateur throughout his career. He played, genuinely, for the love of the game. Of course, in this respect he was lucky. He had the resources to do so. In that sense, he was born what we might now call 'a gentleman'. But he also acted like a gentleman: he was a courteous, even a chivalrous opponent; fair in his methods of attack, honourable in his means of defence, a man who competed at all times not only within the letter, but also within the spirit, of the game.

So much was this so that it would be easy now for the uninitiated to view him not only as an essentially anachronistic, but also as a slightly absurd, character. Then let this be said. None of his team-mates or opponents ever did. True, they all saw a well-mannered man. But most, and those on the receiving end especially, also acknowledged a 'hard', even a 'ruthless' cricketer, one who was naturally 'far too...disciplined to be a bad loser', but who remained 'so firm a believer in winning' that he was actually 'far more dedicated to the task...than most professionals'.[6] In this, if seemingly little else, Peter May much resembled Sir Donald Bradman. Perhaps the greatest of all cricketers, Bradman was an Australian, a country-boy, and a graduate only of the legendary 'university of life'. As such, he was an amateur sportsman in name alone. He held down a 'civilian' job. But cricket was his life. And in his life, he meant to be successful. He was. Indeed, he was the most successful batsman, captain, and cricketer *tout court*, of all time. This success, at the highest level, owed most to sheer talent, and something to back-breaking hard work. But it was also the product of a pitiless competitiveness. As he put it, to his rather more indulgent compatriot Keith Miller,

> When you play Test cricket...you don't give an inch. Play it tough, all the way. Grind them [ie, the opposition] into the dust.[7]

Yet when he retired from the game, in 1948, Bradman preferred to recollect not so much his own batting average as 'an abiding conviction that I...played the game as it should have been played'. Even his country's great successes seemingly meant less to him than 'a host of wonderful friendships', which test cricket had opened up for him.[8]

There was nothing affected in these observations. On the contrary. For the guarantee of their authenticity lay in the seeming paradox of their context. To Bradman, winning friendships by 'playing the game' was perfectly compatible with winning the game by 'playing tough'. Competitiveness and chivalry went together in the cricketing ethic. And so they did too in a gentleman's manners. One might go further. The very definition of a Victorian, an Edwardian, or even an interwar English gentleman lay in his capacity to reconcile a profound competitiveness with a genuine chivalry; thus to render coherent, through his engaged but delicate behaviour, a social ethic which might otherwise have appeared contradictory, even according to its own principles. Moreover, cricket was widely acknowledged as a peculiarly effective vehicle for the fulfilment of this, otherwise elusive, cultural synthesis. The cricketer thus became the very symbol of the 'sportsman', and 'sportsmanship' the very best analogy for the well-lived life.

Decline of manners in sport accompanied by decline in value attached to 'being a gentleman'

That view rings rather hollow today. This is partly the result of our increasing, and increasingly justified, unwillingness to take seriously the claims of the game of cricket as a pleasurable vehicle for the creation and sustenance of good manners. But it is also partly because of our growing, and altogether less fully corroborated, presumption against the very idea of there being such a thing as a *modern* gentleman. For today, the gentleman is, more and more, conceived of as an essentially outdated, and therefore as a preposterous figure. He is, in this understanding, an isolated man, largely confined to 'a few select private zoos called clubs'.[9] He is supposedly possessed of an anachronistic soul, observable from his gratuitously 'fine appearance' and his dysfunctionally 'elegant manners', also through his contempt for 'trade', by his fear of 'work', and finally in his habitual concern for the virtues of his 'ancestors'.[10] Even his love of sport, so often still exemplified in the ready turn of phrase that such and such behaviour 'is just not cricket' is, so it seems, more a tribute to his own uncomprehending failure in the era of contemporary complexities than it is the expression of his power to punish those — all the rest of us — who fail to maintain his ethereal, not to say idle, ideals for living.

Moral values of the gentleman more important in Victorian England than rank or class

In short, we now invariably deride the 'gentleman; because we take him to be the paradigm of the obsolete, and of the immoral, hereditary principle in society. And we deplore his ethic because we understand it to be no more than the elucidation of a leisured purpose in life. But we are wrong. Certainly, our Victorian predecessors would have taken us to be misinformed. On both counts too, for they did not understand cricket to be, either in essence or by habitual practice, 'an organized excuse for loafing'.[11] Rather, they took the first to be the most admirable development of individual character. And they conceived of the second as a particularly efficient instrument for its arduous, as well as agreeable, cultivation. More to the point, their idealism seems to have been much closer to historical truth than our cynicism. For the earliest accounts of the English gentlemen do not designate one of a specific, and hereditary, class.[12] And that fluidity was clearly carried over into early nineteenth-century English life. Tocqueville, for one, noted how universally acknowledged 'gentlemen' of the time were not confined to members of one rank.[13] His contemporary, Baron de Staël Holstein, went further still, observing that whilst being called a gentleman 'is the first condition for attaining respect in England', the acquisition of the name did not necessarily follow from social class, and that a man lacking the necessary moral qualities, however high his birth, would be denied it. Hence the phrase common at that time amongst persons of the lower class, 'though he be a Lord, he is not a gentleman'.[14]

Part of this ambiguity — and transferability — of gentlemanly status was traceable to the relatively easy movement from class to class which most observers pinpointed as one of the peculiar aspects of early-Victorian England.[15] But another, and perhaps the greater part, was the product less of social mobility *per se* than of the cultural consequences of a more general contemporary civilizing process. This was because the Victorians dreamed less off an infinitely elastic, and more of a limitlessly improved society. To be sure, the latter never excluded the former. Ability, effort, even simple good fortune were, according to this scheme of things, properly to be rewarded by social success and in social esteem. But general cultivation was not exhausted by individual well-being in that understanding. If this had been so, then money — simple wealth — would have been quite a sufficient currency for the measurement of contemporary social standing.[16] But it never was. Other qualities counted too. They included rather more subtle, and suitable, general moral values. Indeed, it was precisely because the Victorians remained so conscious of rank, that is, of its surviving and real importance within a society seemingly more and more constructed out of the fruits of individual endeavour, that such ethical qualities — unrelated either to birth or riches — were actually *increasingly* valued at that time. For these qualities — the qualities of a gentleman — transcended *both* rank and achievement. As such, they were able to forge the moral synthesis of modern civility which an increasingly complex, and increasingly sophisticated, industrial society — part aristocratic, part bourgeois, overwhelmingly working-class — desperately needed.[17]

The gentleman's manners provided a common aspiration in a changing society

In other words, as Victorian England changed, as it became an altogether more commercial, more pluralistic, and even a more democratic society, so it demanded a new ethic of social intercourse, specifically one which might replace the old certainties of prescriptive hierarchy with the novel decencies of social quality. At the same time, as it became a much more class-divided society, increasingly rent asunder by the all too obvious discrepancies of wealth, income and power, so it sought solace in a traditional vehicle of common integration, above all in that cultural code which emphasized what united Englishmen rather than in the peculiar customs which tore them apart. In blending the moral and aesthetic dimension of *both* a modern and an ancient way of life, the contemporary cult of the gentleman fulfilled at least part of this complex task. Certainly, the Victorians thought as much. For it was in the 'nineteenth century' that the 'flow of discourses on the gentleman' traceable, albeit exiguously, to Chaucer's time, suddenly became 'a flood'.[18]

These treatises invariably identified not a born, nor not necessarily a born, but a made — or rather a cultivated — man. As the *Quarterly Review* put it, the word 'gentleman' though 'originally' signifying a 'man of family' now applied 'to all those who share the position, manners, cultivation, etc of men of family'.[19] Furthermore, they normally projected the image not of a leisured, and certainly not of an unworldly, but instead of a 'practical...and...industrious' character.[20] More subtly, they usually pointed to a talent for 'agreeability', applicable in all circumstances, between all persons, and achieved through the miracle of treating everyone 'out of the feeling of equality', yet without disregarding the 'varieties of rank' between men.[21] In all this, they characteristically assumed the virtues of courage, courtesy and truthfulness; seemingly, with a special stress on truthfulness.[22] Then they took the sum of these qualities, and pronounced them something peculiarly English: the English gentleman. There was no particular chauvinism in this. Indeed, it was a view with which may foreigners heartily agreed. So much so that some found the word itself impossible to render into their own idiom. As Taine put it, 'We have not the word because [we] have not the thing.[23]

Yet having the 'thing' mattered very much indeed. For this was a code of honour which could convince the aristocrat that his true vocation lay in arduous imperial administration just as it persuaded him that the industrial *parvenu* might be his equal. At the same time, it was an ideal which suggested to the common man that he might actually possess the qualities necessary to win the highest respect, even as he observed the traditional forms of social deference. And, all the while, it was an ethos which promised Englishmen, of all ranks, that they were somehow superior to foreigners; not just simply because of who they were, certainly not because of their genetic make-up, nor even on account of their military prowess, but owing to the manner in which they *behaved* — towards others and towards each other.

Sport, especially cricket, rather than education or religion, united England

But why was it exclusive to the English? Or, more precisely, how had the English come to learn its tenets so well? Because of their games. Above all, because of cricket. Scholarly tracts, after all, attracted only the few. Public schools instructed barely a few more. Even evangelical religion reached little further down the social order than the shopkeeping classes. Sport alone comprehended the whole nation.[24] And just one sport engaged all of the people. This was cricket: 'in every sense a game of the people generally, from the highest to the lowest', an exercise which 'enjoy[ed] the attention of the prince and [of] the peasant' as it kept up 'the manly character' of both of them, even indeed as it

> associated together the active, the ardent and the dextrous of every grade....encourag[ing] a friendly feeling between partners at other times widely separated [yet] without destroying the respect and deference due to rank and wealth.[25]

It is easy to smile at the expression of such sentiments; more important to acknowledge just how much truth they contained. Early nineteenth-century cricket was a sport of kings: Frederick, Prince of Wales, son of George II, was a known enthusiast. It was also the game for gentlemen. Frederick's contemporary, the Duke of Bedford, was a keen participant. Finally, it was the pastime of the plebs. Think of Alfred Mynn. True, the public schools took it up, civilized and sanitized, during the 1860s and afterwards. Yet just at the moment that they did so, a 'race of professionals' arose from the primitive, gambling, sideshow to form the backbone of the county championship, or first-class game, of late Victorian England. Hence the game's tone, albeit refined, remained varied. And cricket clubs, soon associated with 'every religious, social and business organisation…of any size', continued to reflect the diversity of those institutions well into the twentieth century.[26]

This diversity alone explains the popularity of the game, as well as the intensity with which it was followed. Thus the Eton versus Harrow match was conceived by later-Victorian connoisseurs to amount to nothing less than the 'annual climax of the history of mankind'.[27] By contrast, England's victory over Australia in 1926, enabling it to regain the Ashes, drew larger crowds on to the streets of London than at any time since the Armistice.[28] Being so intensely popular, it also commanded peculiar personal commitments, right across the social (and political) spectrum, these often quite openly acknowledged. So George Nathaniel Curzon was happy to admit, even in the first flush of ministerial office, that he invariably consulted the day's cricket scores before ascertaining any of the other news. Similarly, Clement Attlee, of a later generation and still more elevated rank, is alleged never to have bothered, when consulting the daily press, with non-cricketing items at all.[29]

Cricket an essential ingredient of 'Englishness'

Yet it remained defiantly English, or at least English-speaking, in its appeal. The Victorians were boisterously clear on this matter. For them, cricket may have travelled 'wherever her Majesty's servants have carried victorious arms' but 'no single cricket club' had ever 'dieted on frogs, sauer-kraut or macaroni'.[30] Even later, gentler, chroniclers agreed. Hence for Neville Cardus, it remained a curious fact that 'none except the people of England, or the English-speaking countries has excelled at cricket'.[31] This was a fact which bound those countries, almost 'romantically', together.[32] It was also a truth increasingly crucial to the way in which cricket, from the 1860s onwards, came to embody a set of values, 'of mind, spirit and body' on which the very 'life of the nation', so it seemed, was 'based'. These values, in turn, transformed the game from simply being the most popular pursuit of Englishmen into something like 'the right of all Englishmen', even into a critical aspect of 'the development of each [Englishman] into a "gentleman"'.[33]

How? For some, the process seemed so natural as to be beyond serious consideration. Arthur Waugh, Hampstead man of letters, and father of writers Alec and Evelyn put it so: 'With a thorough knowledge of the Bible, Shakespeare and Wisden [the cricket almanac] you cannot go far wrong'.[34] This as advice to a family friend aspiring, at the time, to a literary career. Most were not prepared to go quite that far. For them cricket, only semi-humorously understood as 'the Englishman's religion', was important precisely because, unlike the Church of England, it was a game patronized by all Englishmen and at the same time only by Englishmen. This, seemingly simultaneous, generic universality and ethnic exclusivity was vital to its cultural dimension as a vehicle for the physical, mental and moral improvement of Englishmen, *qua Englishmen.* For it made cricket quite different from football, a game which the English gave to the world, only to be confounded by the world; and also from tennis, a game which retained peculiar and exclusive connotations all around the world.[35]

Twin elements of natural talent and rigorous application led to practice and patience rather than flashy showmanship

But there was something else too. Cricket became an instrument of general moralisation not simply because it was popular but rather because it was complex. Indeed, such improvements of the national character as it promised were, at least in the first instance, a function of the game's own highly sophisticated organizational, requirements. At the risk of some over-simplification, these may be described as the necessity of individual skill; a division of labour; and social co-operation. Their cultural fruits included the qualities of personal modesty; appreciation of others; and generosity towards one's opponents.

Few of cricket's pioneers, and still fewer of its later connoisseurs, doubted that it was a game which demanded the highest degree of individual ability: quickness of eye, fleetness of foot, timing allied to strength, aggression complemented by patience. This was scarcely surprising. It did, and still does. Moreover, in that respect, it was and is scarcely different from any other competitive sport. Yet, even in this respect, cricket's first serious students also noted in it certain important qualifications to the realm of pure talent. First, the game's skills were actually *best* deployed modestly, and certainly shorn of all 'superfluous flourish'. For instance, in the case of batting, unnecessary showmanship was actually 'fatal to good timing'. It might 'appear very graceful to ladies', and to 'spectators as do not understand the game'. But to the real 'cricketer's eye' it was not only 'meretricious' but also 'dangerous'. In this way, the minimum of associated display was actually deemed essential to the maximum of real effectiveness.[36]

Secondly, even the greatest natural ability seldom alone sufficed. For cricket was an essentially artificial activity, which therefore had to be mastered, or learned. This implied a certain degree of intelligence. Early accounts were clear on this matter. Thus Charles Cowden Clarke: 'A man who is stupid will not make a fine cricketer'.[37] It also required a considerable body of knowledge. So much so that Edwardian students of its finer points spoke quite unselfconsciously about 'the science of the game'. Nor were these scholars just non-playing swots. The great Ranjitsinhji frequently referred to important and influential 'schools of cricket'. It is quite clear that he equally frequently consulted them. Similarly, that he did so in order to *practice* the arts they divulged: this was because there was 'no short cut to good cricket'. On this all contemporary (and subsequent) authorities agreed. Thus for the gifted Indian prince, as much as for any 'ordinary mortal', a regime of 'careful, patient and whole-hearted practice' was 'the only royal road'.[38]

Importance of teamwork in encouraging forbearance and individual self-sacrifice

The morality of practice assumed the virtue of patience. But it also taught the more subtle ethic of forbearance. This was important. Indeed, for some earlier chroniclers the capacity to 'bear and forbear' was no less than 'one of the essentials of a true cricketer'. This was true for the rather obvious reason that a batsman 'must often lose his cricket, but not his good humour'.[39] It was also true for the altogether less obvious reason that a bowler often relied upon others, namely fielders, who might not only let him down, but who might do so *all the worse* if he (the bowler) could not control his emotions. Tom Richardson, the great Surrey and England fast bowler explained:

> One essential every bowler who has any pretension to the name must possess — a perfectly equitable temper ... to have laid a trap for the batsman, him lured on to ruin...and then see the ball drop out of the fieldsman's hands...it is at this moment that the philosopher must prevail over the man...a hasty exclamation of disgust [and] the fieldsman is spoilt for the day.[40]

If that now sounds a little precious (though Richardson was the least precious of men), it pointed to another, and perhaps still profounder, aspect of cricket's moralizing régime. This was the division of labour. For cricket was then, as now, a game of specialists. True, there were and are real 'all-rounders' in the game; exceptionally skilled and practised men capable of performing the arts of batting, bowling and fielding to the highest standard. But they were rare. The norm was specialist batsmen and specialist bowlers. (Specialist fielders at the highest level were, and are, unknown.) This was unremarkable in itself, and scarcely differentiated cricket from any other team game. With this important qualification: as everyone seems to have agreed, most young men really *wanted* to be batsmen. This was because batting was more fun, more exhilarating, and somehow even more glorious. As such, it exerted a 'fascination' all 'of its own', one which appealed 'with especial vehemence' to 'ninety-nine out of every hundred cricketers'.[41]

And that was a problem. For it was self-evident that no such proportion of players, in any balanced and thus successful team, could be batsmen. So, some were going to have to sacrifice their most fervent personal aspirations in order to fulfil the collective good. This was partly a matter of individual discovery, of finding out which of the specialist skills each budding cricketer excelled at. It was also partly a matter of social class. As Richardson lamented, the 'natural' preference for bat over ball was especially marked 'in the case of amateurs'.[42] But this was never exclusively the case. The fastest of Victorian pace-bowlers, C J Kortright, was an amateur, a gentleman, and an exemplar of the idle rich who proudly boasted that he 'never worked a day in his life'.[43] Alternatively, the greatest of all post-Edwardian batsmen, J B Hobbs, was a model professional, drawn from working-class stock, who scarcely enjoyed a moment of rest.[44] In fact, most of all, it was a matter of fitting particular attributes to common purposes. In short, cricket demanded of each cricketer that, regardless of his wishes, regardless even of his abilities, he be a good 'team-man'. It might almost have invented the phrase. Certainly, it popularized the concept.

That might seem a trivial point. However, few contemporary observers believed so. One, Jean Fayard, thought that this feature of cricket — in itself — explained the failure of the French to take up the game. In his own words:

> If the French were to play cricket, they would all want to be batsmen — the cynosure of all eyes — at the same time, just as nearly all of them want to be Prime Minister.[45]

So widespread was this understanding, even — one might say particularly — amongst Frenchmen themselves that the very willingness of Englishmen to sacrifice themselves in this way came almost to define the national spirit in what was increasingly taken to be the English national game. Indeed, some of their less observant compatriots came to think of it as the *only* game that Englishmen played. '*J'adore ce cricket — c'est tellement anglais*' remarked Sarah Bernhardt one day, on being taken to watch a game of football.[46]

Importance of informal sanctions rather than rigid legislation

More remarkably still, successful cricket required that opponents co-operate almost as much as team members. For it was a 'rough and ready' game, in the sense that its rules, though specifically designed to make competition fair, were themselves far from fallible. They were incomplete. There were, 'as all cricketers knew, a thousand and one problems…for which the laws do not provide'. And even insofar as they were comprehensive, they were not necessarily unambiguous. The fabled Rule 42, on intimidatory fast bowling, required and requires careful interpretation, both of the batsman's capabilities and the bowler's intentions, by the umpire. Finally, even to the degree that they were clear, they were and are seldom easy to enforce. Hence the umpire was deemed not merely to be infallible but also, paradoxically, understood to be vulnerable; and a *true* cricketer was presumed not simply to be at all times properly respectful of his decisions, which were 'final, above suspicion' and 'beyond criticism', but also necessarily to be helpful in the performance of his (the umpire's) task, willing for instance to gainsay an umpire's decision *to his own disadvantage* (the cricketer's, that is) if honesty demanded it.[47]

From these, essentially technical, imperatives the characteristic manners, that is, the wider cultural benefits of cricket gradually flowered. 'Personal modesty' was the polite adjunct of individual talent. The more talented the player, the more properly modest about it. Rooted in the notion that skill was actually more *effectively* deployed without display, it elevated the calculating absence of self-regard to the dutiful virtue of self-abnegation. No-one ever put it more trenchantly than Bobbie Burlton, author of the definitive study of *Cricketing Courtesy*:

> Don't "play act". There is all the difference in the world between showing-off and general gusto. Cricket and cheerfulness should be inseparable, but the quietly witty characters in the game are

rare birds. You may be a wit, but if you are not, facetiousness annoys many more than it pleases, and what is considered as funny by a handful of perhaps not very intelligent spectators may not really be awfully amusing.[48]

Importance of acknowledging the achievements of others

On the other hand, as Burlton well knew and related properly, no cricketer should fail to acknowledge others' recognition of his achievement. This was especially true of successful batsmen. Clapped by the crowd, as they usually were (and still are) on reaching each 50, they were required 'by courtesy' and as a matter of 'good manners' to 'acknowledge the people's pleasure by at least touching [their] cap if…wearing one or by raising [their] bat if…not'.[49]

'Appreciation of others' meant the proper recognition by players of the importance of fellow team members as essential contributors to their own success and enjoyment. Implied in the division of labour, and entailed in the doctrine of 'team spirit', this duty took the form of specific and various rules for good, social, etiquette. For instance,

> A mild apology to your captain if a rank bad…ball is treated with great discourtesy by the batsman and to your wicketkeeper if he allowed byes because you quite unintentionally bowled a ball wide of the leg stump.

Or, more simply, still

> When you have taken a wicket by means of a catch or a stumping, thank the fielder responsible. He will appreciate it.[50]

Thereby to show

> how this, the most…individual…of all our [team] games, should and can be completely unselfish in its conduct.[51]

But there was more to it than that. For in the generosity of mutual opponents cricket actually promoted good-will amongst *all* protagonists. This was a virtue implied in the necessity of competitive co-operation. It was embodied in the doctrine of fair play. But, once more, it assumed the guise of many, particular and required, gestures of mutual regard. Naturally, it meant not taking any unfair advantage of one's (temporary) adversaries. Hence

> If you accidentally baulk or interfere with a fielder [whilst] batting

> and either directly or as a result of overthrows runs result, apologise to the fielder and do not take the runs.[52]

It also suggested an appreciation of his very presence.

> So those off shouted words — "man in" — signalled to fielders that they should rise and applaud the "new arrival" to the crease, after the fall of each wicket. This was a "compliment" to his potential contribution to the game, however small it might prove to be, or indeed the fielding team actually wished it to be.[53]

Finally, it required the acknowledgement of his achievements. Most poignantly of all, from the bowler who had just received the ultimate punishment. Thus

> Another of cricket's delightful habits is the applause by the fielding side for a six. If you are the bowler who enables the good hit to happen, be the first in your applause.[54]

Personal modesty, appreciation of others and generosity towards one's opponents added up to a régime of good manners. As such, they represented not only these 'further occasions' from which 'manners maketh man' but actual proof that the making of a well-mannered man was possible within the realm of cricket alone.[55] Put another way, a good cricketer was a 'good sportsman'. And a 'good sportsman' was a good, that is a well-mannered, man. For this reason, the significance of being acknowledged as a good sportsman, especially through the medium of being a cricketer, was appreciated far beyond the confines of cricket itself. Indeed, it is no exaggeration to suggest that as cricket gradually established itself as the national game in England after about 1860, so the specifically cricketing virtues became virtually synonymous with 'sportsmanship' more generally in the English mind; and, more strikingly still, so 'sportsmanship' thus defined became virtually synonymous with the simple fact of being English, *tout court*, both in native — and even in foreign — estimations of the race.

The Bodyline tour: adherence to rules not sufficient to evince true sportsmanship

None of this made Englishmen of the time easy losers. Nor even did it ensure their sportsmanship. Consider the famous case of its (alleged) breach. This occurred in the so-called 'Bodyline' tour, by MCC (the English team) of Australia in 1932-3. During that series, the England captain, Douglas Jardine, repeatedly deployed the tactic of 'leg-theory', or the use of his fastest bowlers (most especially Harold Larwood) in a particularly aggressive manner, directing them to aim short, fast-pitched balls, delivered from over the wicket and spearing in from the leg-side, to the batsman's midriff, throat and even head. The speed, the accuracy and (frankly) the effectiveness of this method of attack soon led to considerable bad-feeling amongst the participants. Then, when bad blood passed into real injuries, harsh feelings erupted. And at Adelaide, in January 1933, they provoked something akin to an international incident.

First, W M Woodfall was seriously hurt by one of Larwood's express, and vicious, deliveries. Then, as the England manager, Sir Pelham Warner, offered his commiserations, Woodfall dismissed him with the [in]famous words

> I don't want to see you, Mr Warner. There are two teams out there. One of them is trying to play cricket and the other is not.[56]

More important, however, was the nature of the accusation made against Jardine, which the Australian Board addressed to the MCC immediately afterwards. Its historic cable spoke of Bodyline 'menacing the best interests of the game, causing bitter feelings between the players and threatening relations between the countries'. But most crushing of all was the observation that 'in our opinion it (ie, Bodyline) is unsportsmanlike'.

Crushing but also immediately counter-productive; for it was that accusation — and not the potential diplomatic incident — which concerned the MCC. Ironically, Jardine feared that the authorities might not support him. But Gubby Allen, his vice-captain assured him that they would. Why? Because 'no-one could call an Englishman unsporting with impunity'. Allen was proved right. MCC quickly replied, 'deplor[ing]' the Australian Board's 'cable'. Then, they expressed their support for the captain and his manager. Finally, and most pointedly of all, they insisted on the withdrawal of the word 'unsportsmanlike'. The Australian Board capitulated. Retraction of the insult came before the fourth test. The games continued. So too the tactics. England won the series handsomely. But quietly, they acknowledged the force of the Australian's case. Jardine never captained England against Australia again. Larwood's test career was brought to a complete halt. 'Bodyline' was surreptitiously outlawed. Hypocrisy? Certainly. English pride was dubiously sustained. But, more importantly, cricket's reputation was saved. Most importantly of all, the notion that 'sportsmanship' counted above everything — even above maintaining cordial relations between the two countries — was upheld.[57]

The modesty and sincerity developed by cricket expected in every sphere of behaviour

To understand why this was so is, accordingly, to appreciate just how elevated a position the institution of cricket, and through it the characteristic notion of sportsmanship, had come to occupy in the typical post-Victorian English mind. In part, it is to perceive how cricket, so organized and so motivated, gave to its practitioners the moral fruits of what the game's technical imperatives demanded from them. The reserved display of talent produced genuinely modest men. Certainly, there was nothing affected, nothing false, in Peter May's outward demeanour. A co-operative endeavour sustained really appreciative team-mates. No-one ever doubted Tom Richardson's words when he said 'sorry', nor when he said 'thank you'. And a necessary indulgence to the needs of faithful opponents undoubtedly gave birth to generations of generous rivals. That is what Bradman meant by the 'wonderful friends[hip]' which had come from playing the game as it 'should' have been 'played'.

But it is also to conceive how cricket could, and did, become something very much more than that. Demanding the highest degree of natural talent, yet positively requiring that such ability be sparingly displayed; necessitating the greatest willingness to sacrifice personal ease for diligent achievement, yet normally ensuring that common needs were placed above individual concerns; finally, offering the enchanting possibilities of worldly renown, yet subtly subordinating them all for national pride, the game of cricket became, in effect, a metaphor for life of the Edwardian and post-Edwardian English gentleman. First, it described, at least by analogy, much of what he actually did. Then it depicted, often all too clearly, how he understood himself. Then, it suggested, whether to his associates or his subordinates, how the world might profitably understand him: that is, how it might understand him as a *cricketer*. For to be a cricketer was to be a man of skill, determination, and honour; at once physically vigorous but also mentally alert; hard-working but naturally graceful with it; above all, competitive but also charitable, a man in pursuit of life's prizes but always able to treat each of life's other pursuers as his equal, even as his friend.

Sporting metaphors and their influence on the vocabulary of normal behaviour

At its most superficial, cricket achieved this miracle of symbolic dominion by a kind of linguistic invasion of everyday life. Cricketers, cricket-lovers and even the general public came gradually to conceive of many, then most and occasionally, all the vagaries of life, whether natural or contrived, in peculiarly cricketing terms. Thus to be granted three-score years and ten was to have had a 'good innings'. Or the pilgrim's progress was recounted in 'playing a straight bat'. Even time's winged chariot discovered a cricketing aspect:

> Life's a game of cricket
> We score away quite fast,
> But cruel death sends in a shot
> And bowls us out at last.[58]

But at its more significant, cricket assumed the function of a genuinely civilizing medium, an instrument through which individuals, societies and mankind generally became gentler. In all this, of course, there was an element of *noblesse oblige*. And the game of gentlemen, was often understood to be a vehicle through which the privileged classes might assuage the passions of the mass of the people, simply so it seemed through the act of condescending to play them at cricket, every now and then. Such was, and possibly still is, the underlying rationale of the legendary village cricket match.[59] Certainly it was, and still is, the defining principle of its all too numerous fictional accounts. Little else can explain G M Trevelyan's famous observation that

> If the French [nobility] had been capable of playing cricket with the peasants, their chateaux would never have been burnt.[60]

Importance of lessons of sportsmanship in fostering shared values: the British Empire's adoption of cricket

Something rather more came from the responsibilities of empire. Too often these efforts, and their cricketing fruits, have been derided as little more than colonial bread and circuses. But a matter of historical record, cricket went to the colonies less to suppress other nations than to encourage them to *co-operate amongst each other*. This was especially true, for instance, of British India. There, Lord Harris encouraged a diverse Indian youth to play cricket together. Parsees, Hindus and Muslims were brought together as never before under its auspices, much to the benefit of their health and morale. It is easy now to sneer at such efforts. It would be easier still to discover in them the key to a dastardly imperialist plan to subvert the (supposedly) otherwise radical impulses of a proto-nationalist youth. For that reason, it is all the more important to recall that it was under Harris's patronage that P Baloo, an 'untouchable', initially broke through into major cricket, later going on to become the most successful bowler on the first All-India tour of England.[61]

But most of the impetus for moralizing improvement of this sort came neither from the desire to placate nor from the imperative to rule. It derived from the simple capacity of the game to break down social barriers. Paradoxically, this was true even of those aspects of the game which seemed to emphasize them. Think of the 'gentlemen versus players' (amateurs against professionals) match. This contest was begun as early as 1806. It lasted until 1962, over 100 years.[62] To be sure, it reflected the social divisions of the game. Yet it also acknowledged the sheer diversity of the people who played it. Moreover, it symbolized the degree to which *all of them* were bound within the framework of a genuinely national and popular game in which the civilizing process, and the gentlemanly virtues, were truly disseminated across all social classes, and through which — in the negotiation of social class by cricket — a 'classless' gentleman could, and did, flourish in modern Britain.

Classless not in the sense of possessing no social class; that self-delusion was recognized for the nonsense it was and is. But classless in the sense of recognizing the qualities of a gentleman in individuals, regardless of their social class. The blessed, in this sense, were those who by personal subscription to, individual performance of, and wider acceptance in a code of honour, won the unambiguous standing of gentleman. They did exist. Think of Jack Hobbs. And their existence ensured for every 'good cricketer', personally renowned or not, something of the title of gentleman in England, between about 1850 and 1950; conversely that understanding made every 'good gentleman' at least something of a cricketer. As the then Roman Catholic Archbishop of Liverpool, Dr R Rowney put it, just after the Second World War,

If Stalin had learned to play cricket, the world might be a better place to live in.[63]

Sport important not only as a diversion, but as a civilizing influence

Conventional wisdom demands that we scoff at such sentiments today. Similarly, it insists that we acknowledge the supposedly class-based origins of cricketing morality, the cruel divisive segregation of cricketers into 'gentlemen' and 'players' prior to 1962, the anachronistic unwillingness of the authorities to appoint a professional captain of England before 1952, the various legends of Lord Hawke's social snobbery, and the rest.[64] If so, then conventional wisdom has missed something which Japanese students, and even Premier Mugabe, have seen: that cricket, owing to its peculiar nature and because of its potential popularity, can be a vehicle for something more important than itself. To be sure, it is only a game. And even in its modern vicious, professional, dispensation it is only one of the many available entertainments for the amusement of the masses. But, properly organized, carefully guided and manfully defended, it can stand for something more than gamesmanship. It can create a nation of gentlemen. It once did. Intelligent observers — elsewhere — believe it still might.

There is no need to be sentimental about this observation in order to perceive its underlying truth. Real enthusiasts for the game rarely were. Thus the protagonists of C P Snow's *The Search*, musing upon 'cricket' as 'the perfect efflorescence of Edwardian England', calling it the 'finished product' of a 'great civilization', never shirked from the simultaneous realization that it was also an 'expensive, luxurious [and] wasteful' ritual, with a 'slice of viciousness running through [it]'. In this way it was, so they concluded, much like Russian ballet, itself the 'perfect efflorescence of [Tsarist] Europe', but an activity 'artistically dignified on the surface [yet] with a lot of sheer vulgarity underneath'.[65]

Much, but not quite like. Commenting on this passage, the premier historian of English decadence observes that, whilst insightful, it is not strictly correct. For cricket, though like ballet in some respects, and though indeed 'a sumptuous ritual celebrating beauty and style…grace and youth' was, in other regards, quite different from the effete European art. The latter was altogether more aesthetic, more sexual and more fantastic. The former, by dint of its secondary phenomena — the team spirit, the village green, the school training, the afternoon outdoors — led its practitioners back from individual connoisseurship to social responsibility. The ritual of ballet was 'insubordinate, implicitly in revolt against...seriousness'; that of cricket was 'completely subdued to, subordinate to, the large rituals of "life" — serious things like government and marriage'.[66]

That is why young Evelyn Waugh hated cricket and loved ballet. And it is why those in search of virtue should do the opposite. At the very least, it is why they cannot be indifferent to the slow death of the game in our schools and colleges. For the sources of good manners amongst men are always various, and seldom traceable only to the most obvious sources. It goes without saying that the manners of a gentleman are best learned at home, or possibly at school, and always by prolonged, educated habituation. But not everyone either has, or ever had, the privilege of a decent home, a good school, or extended reflection on the matter. Some always did, and always will, rely on rougher sources for their training in civilization. The Victorians, and their immediate successors, appreciated this. We, it seems, do not. They galvanized a truly popular sport to serious moral ends. We have effectively repudiated that quest. There is no reason to believe that we have gained as a result.

7

Flirting and Deferring

Southern Manners

John Shelton Reed

Southern manners clearly identifiable as distinct from American norm

Whilst the first few chapters of this book have dealt with universal truths of civil behaviour and moral education, they may seem (particularly in the last chapter, for those unfamiliar with the nuances of cricket) overly reliant on the example and history of English manners. This is not perhaps entirely surprising: several authors have drawn attention to the problems that France as a nation might have with some of the manners and modes of behaviour discussed so far. But there is one other and obvious seat of the sort of European-American manners examined by this book, and it is one with a distinct tradition which can be seen as having incorporated and transformed certain aspects of the European tradition of manners and, some might argue, provided for them a route into other areas of the United States. The manners of the South are clearly identifiable and maintain the — at first sight contradictory — idea of democratic manners.

The idea of democratic manners has puzzled observers (when they haven't simply assumed the phrase is a contradiction in terms) since Tocqueville. I want to suggest that such a thing exists and that it can still be found in the American Republic, if only in what has been notoriously the nation's least democratic corner — that is, the lower right. Let me start with a story.

One day my friend Dick, a history professor at the University of North Carolina, was riding in a New York airport limousine when it stopped to pick up another passenger, an elderly lady burdened with luggage and confronted by a garden gate that wouldn't open. After watching her struggle for a while, Dick got out and gave her a hand.

When they were settled in the car the lady thanked him. The driver (who had watched everything from behind the wheel) said, 'He's from the South'.

I find that a delicious story, not least because my friend is a Midwesterner who came to North Carolina via Harvard and Oxford, and he's about as Southern as — oh, say, as T S Eliot. This suggests how careful we should be about generalizing, but it also tells us that Americans still think that Southern manners are different from the American norm.

Manners as friendliness: feigned or genuine but noticeable

And of course they are different. A student told me recently about her new neighbours, a Jewish couple from Los Angeles, who were mightily offended when a new acquaintance asked them casually where they go to church. Although this is still a standard gambit in the South, no offence intended, just a way of figuring out who you're dealing with (and 'We're Jewish' is a perfectly satisfactory response), apparently Californians feel it's none of our business. You know, though, Californians have their own intrusive ways. We lived out yonder for a year, and I was offended when people asked (as they often did) what I do for exercise. For starters, coughing a lot is about the extent of my exercise programme these days. Besides, I tend to agree with Robert Frost:

> After babyhood self-improvement becomes a private matter.
> Physical mental or moral, please attend to it where I cant see you
> if you care to avoid my disgust.

(That's the old New Englander's own punctuation or lack of it.)

Anyway, Southern manners really are different, and Southerners usually think they're better, too. Many Yankees agree, but some don't. Sometimes the problem is just that they're not used to us. A student from Philadelphia told our campus paper that when he first came to North Carolina, 'everybody was almost too friendly to me. I didn't know how to react to it'. Another Northern student agreed: 'It ain't easy for a boy from the Bronx to be yessired by cops and cashiers and smiled at by total strangers'. This lad was especially nonplussed by a convenience store clerk who 'thanked me with an earnestness that would have been excessive if I had offered to donate a kidney to her sickly grandmother'.

Most immigrants come to like this sort of thing, in time. But a few observe that manners disguise Southerners' real feelings. (That would sound familiar to the Japanese, of course. They're polite, too, and they get called 'inscrutable'.) 'Southerners are more apt to say cordial greetings to each other, but that's about all', a kid from Illinois told the paper. 'It's a very superficial friendliness'. Some Northerners who have figured this out like it anyway. A graduate student from Boston observed that Southerners' greater friendliness 'works two ways'. 'Some of them are friendly' he said, 'and some of them are but really aren't. It's just sort of a politeness'. But, he added, 'that's fine because it makes things easier anyway'. A Massachusetts businessman agreed. Recalling the years he spent in the South, he said, 'A lot of Northerners thought the Southerners' friendship was phoney — saccharine, sugar-coated. But I didn't care. I'd rather people be nice to me than not nice. If you're going to be the new person in town, the South is a good place to land'.

A few transplants, however, seem to be really annoyed by what they see as our lack of integrity. A department-store executive relocated to Georgia from Ohio complained that Southern graciousness 'does not come across as politeness but insincerity'. And a woman from Philadelphia told a North Carolina journalist, 'It's all epitomized by the neo-Southern Bitch. She dresses so damned cute. Who's she think she's fooling? It's all just fluff, and flirt, and manipulation'. The journalist, a Southerner, commented that there was 'definitely no fluff' to this woman. 'She would not flirt or manipulate: say the wrong thing and she'd simply rip your ears off.'

But she may just have resented the response of Northern men to 'fluff, flirt and manipulation'. Most like it. A Boston boy, for instance, said that Southern coeds are 'a lot more refreshing...Down here they have a sweeter image and I like that'. A graduate student from St Louis added that Southern college women 'don't come on as hard. They're much less aggressive in their relationships'.

By and large, Northern women tend to like the manners and style of Southern men, too. A pharmacy student from New Jersey told the student paper that 'Southern guys are more polite and they're more apt to do things like hold open doors. I did enjoy it. I'm liberated but I'm not going to get pissed off if some guy holds the door open for me'. A student from Pennsylvania agreed, adding, 'They don't seem to forget that you're a woman, and that's nice'. (Well, maybe, but a little later the same woman was saying that 'men are much more chauvinistic in the South'.)

Possibility of misunderstanding can accompany differences in manners between strangers

But Southern manners can get you into trouble outside the South. I was talking to a couple of friends once on a corner at DuPont Circle in Washington, when a sorry-looking black wino edged up to us and stood there, not saying a word. My friends, city boys, ignored him. I tried to, but finally I just couldn't stand pretending that the guy simply…*wasn't there*, so I made eye contact, knowing perfectly well that it was a mistake. 'Excuse me, sir', he said, 'but can you help a homeless individual?' (In DC even the bums use the approved euphemisms.)

It was the 'excuse me, sir' that did it. This guy's mama had raised him right. His manners (and mine) scored him my pocket change.

He and I understood each other perfectly well, but more often problems arise because of misunderstanding. In *Southern Ladies and Gentlemen*, for instance, Florence King writes about the trials of a Southern woman in New York:

> When you rattle off a standard Southern thank-you — "Oh, you're just so nice, I don't know what I'd *do* without you!" the Northern man *believes you*! He believes you so much that he follows you home.

I know what she means. I've actually had a similar experience. On an international flight a couple of years ago, I'd been talking with a cute little Japanese-American flight attendant, and was startled to be asked for my phone number. Now, all I'd done was *chat* (honest). I didn't want to be rude, but I'm happily married, so I just made up a number. Besides, he wasn't my type — which is female, for starters. (Sorry. Couldn't resist telling it that way.)

Anyway, these days more and more Southerners have to deal with non-Southerners, and being misunderstood may in time make us as curt, abrupt, and no-nonsense as New Yorkers. But that would be a shame. Our manners have served us well, and not just by making everyday dealings with strangers more pleasant. As W J Cash recognized 50 years ago in *The Mind of the South*, manners are one reason the 'yoke of class' has 'weighed but lightly' in these parts.

Southern manners served as an essential component of social interaction

Of course Cash did not deny that there were class distinctions in the

South — indeed, he emphasized them, as an aspiring intellectual of the 1930s should. But he insisted that there had been an 'almost complete disappearance of economic and social focus on the part of the masses'. Overstatement, perhaps (Cash was inclined that way), but it's hard to deny that there has been nowhere near as much class consciousness in the South as there *should* have been. Cash was right when he observed that among white Southerners, for whatever reason, 'one simply did not have to get on in this world in order to achieve security, independence, or value in one's own estimation and in that of one's fellows'.

Part of the explanation, he believed, lay in Southern manners. The 'kindliness and easiness' of Southern backcountry life became the 'essential kernel' of 'the famous Southern manner'; in the American South, manners governing relations between the classes have served as a 'balance wheel' and 'a barrier against the development of bitterness' — or, you could as easily say, against the development of class consciousness. Again and again, Cash insisted that the Southern etiquette of class has de-emphasized distinctions between rich and poor (just as the etiquette of race continually emphasized the gulf of course). He argued, for instance, that in the Old South the yeoman seldom encountered 'naked hauteur'. The gentleman 'patronize[d] him in such fashion that...he seemed not to be patronized at all but actually deferred to'. Cash concluded that the 'working code of the Old South' was 'in its peculiar way, simply an embodiment of...the old basic democracy of feeling'.

In Cash's view, the Civil War did nothing to alter this 'working code'. Indeed, the experience of war meant that

> the captains knew [even] better how to handle the commoner, to steer expertly about his recalcitrance, to manipulate him without ever arousing his jealous independence.

And the rise of industry in the form of textile mills meant merely that 'the old personal easy relations' of the countryside were brought indoors. 'The baron knew these workmen familiarly as Bill and Sam and George and Dick, or as Lil and Sal and Jane and Lucy' — and so forth. This particular description goes on, and on, and it's easy to make fun of it. But surely we can allow Cash some licence in describing the human face of paternalism, since he was unsparing in his treatment of its defects. In any case, Cash's description was not just a flight of romanticism, grotesquely applied to the textile mill. He was on to something important.

I will not soon forget what a friend said one time, when he stopped off to see us in North Carolina on his way back home to Mississippi from a sociological convention in the North. He had noticed how some sociologists dealt with the staff of the convention hotel. 'Damn Marxists' he said, 'go on and on about "the workers" — and they treat the help like dirt.' He was right, although I think he should have said 'Yankee Marxists', because this is really a regional matter. From a Southern point of view, many New Yorkers — Marxists or not — treat *everyone* like dirt. Southerners, as Cash recognized, usually treat each other as equals, whatever our private opinions (that is, unless we *want* to insult someone).

The necessity for dignity: the fiction of equality and reality of respect in the South

This regional difference, too, can cause problems. If you are working for someone with New York manners, those manners rub your face in the fact of your subordination. Not long ago, my hometown was buzzing with the story of a Yankee newcomer who took a work crew to task for some fault with their work. The workers simply packed up their tools and left him sputtering in mid-criticism. 'Sonofabitch wants to boss you around like he owns you' was thought to be sufficient explanation.

That is a significant phrase isn't it? 'Like he *owns* you.' Could it be that the legatees of a slave society — whether one's ancestors were on the top, bottom, or side — have a special understanding of the importance of independence, dignity, and pride? It makes sense that the fictive equality among white men under Jim Crow was embodied in manners that did not bring into question the other's worth or self-respect. And those manners seem to be outlasting the conditions that gave rise to them; indeed, most white Southerners now extend them to Southern blacks, most of whom seem willing to return the favour.

The South's democratic manners may be threatened, however, and not just by Northern newcomers. In fact, they were already threatened in 1940, as Cash recognized. He acknowledged that the rise of the middle class and the emergence of the second generation of mill owners meant that even then the 'gulf was growing' between Southern workers and their bosses. Many sons and successors of the early industrialists

> had been trained in the tradition of the old close personal relationship between man and master and...often sought to continue it,

but they were so caught up in speculation and the country club that

> the feeling which had lain at the heart of the old notion of paternalistic duty was fast dwindling, leaving only the shell — at the same time that the notion of paternalistic privilege was remaining as strongly entrenched as ever, and even perhaps being expanded.

Cash was deadly on the imported 'Yankee cult of the Great Executive', a way of thinking that often 'cut straight across the tradition':

> Seducing the vanity especially of the young men who had been educated in the Northern business schools, and their imitators, it led them to surround themselves with flunkies and mahogany and frosted glass, with the result that the worker who had been accustomed to walking into the Old Man's office without ceremony could no longer get to them save at the cost of an effort and a servility which were foreign to his temper and tradition.

Tradition of the company as an extended family encouraged loyalty

Well, we have our own business schools now, but there are still Southern enterprises run on the old principles, and those principles still shape the expectations of many Southern workers. A while back I took a class on a field trip to one of the few remaining family-owned textile mills in North Carolina. The trip had been arranged far in advance, but we arrived to find the place virtually shut down. The entire managerial staff and all but a skeleton crew of workers had gone to the funeral of a retired weave-room worker. That mill will not be unionized any time soon.

Just up the road, however, in Winston-Salem, we witnessed an instructive cultural conflict when Reynolds Tobacco merged with Nabisco and acquired a new management team. A bestselling book, *Barbarians at the Gate*, tells the story of Ross Johnson, the Canadian CEO who came to Winston-Salem from Nabisco. Compared to the junk-bond sharks who eventually stripped him of his company and his job, I must say that Johnson comes off as a rather amiable buccaneer, just a guy out of the sales division who liked to fly around the country in private jets and hang out with professional athletes. But his Great Executive style was inconsistent with the old-fashioned Southern corporate culture of RJR. Mr R J Reynolds and his heirs had not exactly led lives of asceticism and self-denial, but they had been managers of the sort Cash described: walking the factory floor, greeting workers by name, inquiring after their families. It was understood that Reynolds executives drove nothing bigger than a Buick. When David Rockefeller came to Winston-Salem for a speech and asked for a limousine, there was none to be found in the entire city. In the 1950s, one worker recalled 'some mornings pulling up beside Mr Whitaker [the president] in his little brown Studebaker. He'd give me a wave and I'd give him a wave back. We were going into work together. We were all after the same thing'.

Ross Johnson, on the other hand, came to work by helicopter. Do you wonder why Winston-Salem never took to him? Folks were especially cruel to his trophy wife, Laurie, a California Girl widely known as 'Cupcake'. (After she and her husband were given honourary degrees by a needy Florida college, she was known as 'Dr Cupcake'.) Johnson got even by moving his corporate headquarters to Atlanta, observing as he left that Winston-Salem was too 'bucolic'. All over town cars sprouted bumper stickers with the legend 'Honk If You're Bucolic'.

But deference must be earned

Sure, there is deference in the South to men of high standing, but it should not be taken for granted, and it depends on a measure of self-deprecation. Cash had that exactly right.

One Yankee who understood how this works was the novelist Owen Wister. In his novel *The Virginian*, Wister shows how men like his hero carried the values and the manners of the Old South to the Western frontier. His character Judge Henry explains that

> the whole secret…lies in the way you treat people. As soon as you treat men as your brothers, they are ready to acknowledge you — if you deserve it — as their superior.

That wasn't a bad way to operate on the frontier, and we Southerners think it's still a pretty good rule.

8

Respecting the Truth

Manners in the Academy

Robert Grant

Manners and style may be luxuries in 'frontier' societies but are essential in academic life

The poor, Dr Johnson observed, are not 'mortified by the mutilation of a compliment'. Strip life down to its essentials, and manners look decidedly like a luxury. Certainly entire societies have managed to survive and flourish without them: the Wild West, 1920s Australia (as depicted in D H Lawrence's *Kangaroo*), Israel (described by a friend of mine, a travel writer and otherwise loyal Jewess, as the rudest place on earth) and of course Yorkshire, whose inhabitants' plain speaking, as they are pleased to call it, is to them a point of pride and a badge of their identity.

Yorkshire apart, these are or were 'frontier' societies: raw, vigorous, relatively classless, grimly and necessarily competitive. But ordinary social manners are hothouse fruits. They flourish only under what, from the standpoint of survival, are artificial conditions: those being, if not necessarily affluence, then at any rate physical security and a certain prevailing self-confidence. Very elaborate manners are probably a sign of decadence, that is, of a society so far corroded by its own educated irony and made doubtful of its unqualified right to exist as to be disinclined (as in Cavafy's 'Waiting for the Barbarians') to defend itself with the necessary ruthlessness.

Such a society, nevertheless, may still plume itself on its own defiant, enduring stylishness. The truly stylish person (and style is unimaginable without manners) values style above life, because his style *is* his life. Without it his merely physical existence is meaningless, and thus not *worth* defending. It is not hard to imagine that Petronius or Oscar Wilde, both of them gentlemen and genuine *arbitri elegantiae*, would not rather have died as they did than save themselves, had they been able to do so, by passing up the chance of either a generous gesture or a sparkling witticism.

Academic life is of course a luxury. Within it, however, manners, or something analogous to them, are a necessity. In *On Liberty* J S Mill justified toleration in everyday social arrangements in the following terms, that if competition in ideas and life-styles (his notorious 'experiments of living') is permitted then the 'truth' is more likely to emerge. The argument has been widely criticized, not least because what matters in everyday opinion is not its truth-value but its fundamental, culturally-definitive property of consensus, which an excessive pluralism is like to erode.[1] To use Gilbert Ryle's distinction, everyday opinion is more like knowing *how* (to behave, etc) than knowing *that* (such-and-such is the case). That is, it is a system of shared cultural attitudes or even aptitudes, to which epistemic considerations are simply inapplicable.

Toleration differs from tolerance in being premised upon (possible) disapproval

But in intellectual life the concept of truth really is applicable. Here Mill's advocacy of toleration looks a lot more plausible. In 'polite' or 'elegant' societies, to speak in Gibbonian idiom, tolerance is generally considered a virtue and a prime requisite in everyday conduct. But tolerance is not the same as toleration. Tolerance is a moral quality, an aspect of an individual's or a society's character, akin in certain respects to easy-goingness or geniality. Almost certainly it will not extend to tolerating everything (treason, cowardice, dishonesty, unmannerliness or indeed intolerance); but generally it denotes a reluctance to be always finding fault, a cast of mind not bent perpetually on disapproval.

Toleration, on the other hand, is a set of political arrangements. It proceeds from the belief that although some things are strongly (and perhaps rightly) disapproved of, there may nevertheless be compelling reasons not to prohibit them. Premised on disapproval, toleration nevertheless sets limits to its scope and freedom of action.[2]

In the intellectual sphere toleration prevails, but with this difference, that science, learning and scholarship are premised not upon disapproval, but rather upon the principled withholding of approval until it has been earned. They are based, that is, upon unsparing criticism and debate, things which in the everyday world would be thought excessively disputatious, needlessly adversarial, even downright offensive. Ordinary social manners are designed to protect the individual's self-esteem, no matter how foolish or misplaced it may be. But intellect is no respecter of sensibilities. One is admitted to the intellectual forum on the tacit understanding that, for so long as one seeks to participate, one will submit uncomplainingly to criticism.[3]

In everyday life tolerance and indeed manners demand that both criticism and debate, and thus the mere mention of certain obviously controversial subjects, be restrained and in some spheres disallowed. Appearances to the contrary, and boring though it may seem to modern tastes, it was actually in the interests of tolerance that old-fashioned clubmen used to put sex, politics and religion conversationally out of bounds. For, as Mill said (without seeing how close it came to justifying intolerance), 'so natural to mankind is intolerance in whatever they really care about'. If we now admit these subjects to casual conversation, it is probably because we no longer care about them.

The scholar's primary obligation is to truth, not to his theories

The point of toleration in the intellectual realm is to ensure a supply of new ideas, and the aim of criticism and debate not to score points but to get at the truth, or as close to it as the particular discipline allows.[4] The academic ethos should be radically distinguished from the openly confrontational set-up in an English court of law, where the aim is simply to win. There, until very recently, neither side was obliged to divulge its evidence to the other in advance. (Not only is there no academic parallel to this, it would be ludicrous if there were. There is one, however, in industrial research and development, and understandably so.) Rightly or wrongly, the supposition is that truth and justice must automatically emerge from the clash of contending claims, irrespective of and unaided by anyone's prior commitment to them (apart from the judge's and the jury's). The lawyer's first and only duty is to his client, so long as he continues to represent him.[5]

The scholar, by contrast, should be committed more to the truth than to his own opinion. But he will still contribute his opinion, knowing that it is only out of competing opinions that truth can emerge. This is like Rousseau's paradox of democracy, to the effect that one may simultaneously will both one's own minority preference and its contrary, that of the majority, to which one has by definition given one's prior consent. Of course (and *pace* post-modernism, pragmatism, *et al*) the academic consensus is not the General Will. It may agree on the relevant facts and the validity of established procedures, but it is powerless positively to decide the truth. But that is because truth is different from policy. Policy is something we make; truth, something we can only aim at, and, if we are fortunate, discover.

Refusal to acknowledge the possibility of objective truth precludes true membership of the academic community

Truth is properly an object of knowledge, not of will or belief. If some things, especially in the 'hard' sciences, are regarded as substantially indisputable, it is not because the consensus has generated the truth, but rather because the truth has compelled the consensus. It is this common allegiance or self-subordination to truth which constitutes the academic community as a community, provides it with an ethic (objectivity), and also approximates it to a society under the rule of law, in that even its most distinguished member is no less subject than the least, and than the community as a whole, to the authority of fact and evidence. Where those alone rule, as ideally they should, the academy is neither a democracy, nor an aristocracy, nor any kind of 'ocracy' proper.

But where they are lacking, and disciples simply kow-tow to the opinions of the eminent, the academy has moved in a political or religious direction. And so it has also when any significant number of its members, irked by their servitude to objectivity and longing for some new revelation, begin to deny even the possibility of truth. I shall examine this phenomenon later, but for the moment let us observe that to deny the possibility of truth or objectivity is to destroy the only rational basis for both debate and consensus, and thus either to exclude oneself from the academic community or, if one already occupies a key position within it, to destroy it too by reducing it to a welter of faction.

For the most part scholarly etiquette is a matter of toleration. It is so obviously functional as to make one doubt whether it really belongs to manners at all (though ordinary manners also clearly have a function, for all that some societies dispense with them). And indeed, as I have suggested, the unconstrained inquiry it facilitates would be out of place in everyday life, where the academic often forgets that others may take exception to the dispassionateness with which, out of mere habit, he discusses things which are precious to them or touch closely on their self-esteem.

Offence is more likely to be given where values rather than facts are in question. In those areas there is more need for the moderating influence of manners. It seems accordingly as if, in the academic and intellectual worlds, manners or etiquette might be less necessary in the 'hard' sciences than in the humanities, where values are unavoidably mixed up with the subject matter. And here I mean not toleration, but real manners, the kind designed to spare sensibilities. There is a place in academic life, albeit smaller than in the everyday world, for everyday courtesies, since even academics are human.

Manners keep in check the petulance and vanity of some academics

In fact, and though their professional ethos officially militates against it, as individuals academics are often more vain, childish and paranoid than the generality of the population. This is hardly surprising given that they have spent most of their formative years hearing how clever they are. Even where, as in science, human values proper are not involved, an academic may still stake his self-esteem and personal reputation upon some pet theory, whence to challenge it is to strike at the very core of his being. If, therefore, academics' efforts are to be steered towards the collective enlightenment which is their sole *raison d'être*, it will be well if manners continue to perform their customary task of soothing inflamed egos and dampening things down all round. They should also prompt us to avoid personal contention in the first place. It was unmannerly and worse of the great Cambridge critic F R Leavis, egged on by his insufferable wife (herself an excellent critic, incidentally), to vilify his colleagues to his students. Such justified resentment as this excited, often in people to whom Leavis owed a considerable debt of gratitude for their early help and support, made next to impossible the intellectual collaboration (or 'common pursuit') which he was so fond of hymning in his writings.[6]

Owing to the nature of its material, scientific discourse can be, and is, constrained by ferociously exacting standards of evidence, argument and proof. These and the corresponding heuristic have evolved by natural selection. They simply 'work' better than any others. One might say that science in this respect is almost self-regulating. There is less leeway for mere opinion, and the whole is less easily corrupted by ideology, than in the humanities. That is why ideology usually tries to pass itself off as science, and also why, in Communist countries, intelligent, scrupulous people nearly always choose to read scientific or technical subjects at university.

It is thus interesting to note that scientists nevertheless invest their procedures, the scientific community, and their commitment to truth and objectivity with a strongly ethical character. A scientific fraud is seen by his colleagues not as a mere failure, filtered out (as he invariably is) by the autonomous, quasi-mechanical workings of the system, but as a villain, a fool and an egotist, deserving of the utmost condemnation and contempt, because he cared more for his personal fame than for the only thing that matters, the truth. (It should be remarked that true scientific fraud is never committed for material gain; indeed it is hard to see how it could be.)

Absence of cast-iron conclusions in arts subjects allows literary theorists to deny the possibility of truth and meaning

The humanities are not nearly so self-regulating, and therefore stand in need of more deliberate self-scrutiny than science. Such a thing, however, guided by a combination of intellectual and ethical standards, is nowadays rarely to be found, at least in literary studies. Where new topics and methods are concerned, there is toleration of a sort, which is one half of what is required, but no serious criticism of them, which is the other. In consequence literary studies have been almost taken over by hyper-politicized, anti-humanist and profoundly anti-academic ideologies, to the extent that anyone rash enough to oppose them or subject them to detailed criticism is likely to find his chances of tenure or promotion severely reduced.[7] (Not everything is tolerated equally.)

A historian who claimed that Napoleon never existed would only make a laughing-stock of himself. But a literary theorist who informs us *ex cathedra* that the author's meaning is irrelevant to our understanding of a 'text', or is radically indeterminable, or that there is no such thing as meaning anyway, or that philosophy is only another kind of 'writing', or that literary meanings and values are disguised instruments of bourgeois (male, white, Western, etc) 'power', may expect, so long as he swathes these contentions in sufficiently inflated, rebarbative gobbledegook, to find himself rewarded with fame and fortune.

Fashionable literary theory composed of sophistries considered ridiculous by most philosophers

It may be asked how such sophistries (which are almost entirely self-refuting) rose to their current near-orthodoxy. First, to speak in Popperian terms, they are unfalsifiable. They impugn in advance the good faith, and thence the possible value, of any criticism which might be mounted against them (something which also makes them exceptionally unmannerly). Secondly, though still very much a minority creed, they have successfully exploited both literary scholars' intellectual diffidence, and worse, their traditional good manners. It is both right and profitable to give new ideas a hearing, but a *trahison des clercs* not to subject them to criticism.

Contemporary Franco-American literary theory (which is what I have been describing) may in part owe its success precisely to a lack of *appropriate* criticism. For 'theory' (as it is now called for short) is mostly a bundle of ancient philosophical heresies, which, with a few distinguished exceptions (including M H Abrams, Brian Vickers and A D Nuttall), literary scholars have not generally felt themselves competent to refute. But as the ballyhoo surrounding Jacques Derrida's Cambridge degree illustrated, all they needed to do is observe the near-universal contempt in which 'theory' is held by philosophers. If literary academics felt unable to criticize it, they should have been equally cautious about admitting it to consideration in the first place.

Let us return to value and the humanities. The humanities are not everyday life, but an academic study. Nevertheless, they are much closer than the natural sciences to everyday life, since it forms part of their subject matter.[8] Nothing is harder or more important than persuading the humanities student to suspend his everyday values so that he may consider the world, not as it affects his interests (and lofty as they may sound, values are among one's interests), but as it is in itself. The point, of course, is to open up his imagination to the possibility that others have different values and thus construe the world differently. It is also to make him see that truth and objectivity are values too.

Pursuit of truth in academic life makes good behaviour essential

This shift of perspective is desirable in the interests, not of ecumenism, relativism, pluralism, internationalism, cultural self-flagellation or guilt-stricken Third-Worldery generally, but simply of rational understanding. It does not require that we positively abandon our own cultural understanding, values and perspective. Indeed, it may well persuade us that they are inescapable, since our very impulse to transcend them is actually part of (and unique to) our Western cultural inheritance. Furthermore, without the requisite sympathy for our own cultural experience there is much that we shall simply not understand,

and nuances that we shall miss, when we come to study it. If *Verstehen* is necessary to our grasp of other cultures, it is no less necessary to a grasp of our own. What the true academic outlook demands is something both rare and delicate: a disinterestedness that is neither indifference nor disenchantment,[9] and a realization from the outset that truth is nearly always less than absolute, and our approach to it at best asymptotic.

If we are interested in 'truth', as in scholarly discourse we ought to be, we need a modicum of decent behaviour, otherwise debate is impossible. And we must have debate, because truth is not generally vouchsafed to individuals singly. This is not to say that everything must be constantly subjected to criticism. If nothing were ever taken for granted, so that (say) the efficacy of established procedures or the value of criticism itself were continuously to be put in question, either no intellectual enterprise would ever get started, or any that did would soon become a bear-garden.[10]

The craving for certainty all too easily disguises itself as a love of truth. Too impetuous a pursuit of truth leads first to error, and eventually to tyranny of some kind. Burke said it was possible to hate evil too much. So it is to love truth too much. In reality, he who does so does not love it enough. One should love truth, passionately if you like, but not greedily. Truth matters, not because I possess it, but solely for its own sake. There is a parallel here with sentimentality. The craving for certainty leads us away from the world as it exists independently of our self-centred desire, and into the realms of fantasy.[11] In intellectual matters we must always be ready, and if we really care about the truth we shall be happy, to be proved wrong. That, if you like, is Popper's falsifiability-criterion, recast in ethical terms.

Manners amongst scholars prevent prejudice and protect free speech

Academic manners, or the academic ethic, inhibit the natural rush to judgment. The latter, prejudice in short, is no doubt evolutionarily advantageous in practical life. In primitive times, at least in matters of life and death, one must regularly have had to judge by appearances, since there will seldom have been time for deliberation. That reinforces the point made earlier, that from the standpoint of survival academic life is very much a luxury. Academic manners enjoin us to dissemble the intensity of our concern for truth out of the obligation to allow others their say. And it is precisely by allowing others their say that our own certainties are weakened, and the real truth reinforced, that certainty is nearly always premature.

As Matthew Arnold and Cardinal Newman stressed, there is here an overspill into everyday life and culture at large. We used to send people to universities for what, even if it was scientific, was called a liberal education. An induction into academic culture was thought to have a beneficial effect on the character, and such a character to have a beneficial effect on the world, once its owner had returned to it. When we speak of an educated person we mean more than merely that he is intellectually skilled, possessed of a given type and quality of information, and so on. We attribute to him a certain conversability, a readiness to listen to anything decently presented and not manifestly absurd, various types of quasi-moral restraint, and the like.

'High culture' characterized by liberal, and therefore tolerant, behaviour

Such a character displays what may be called liberality of mind. When shared by a significant number of people it amounts to an entire sub-culture. (Though I shall later call it 'liberal culture', it should be distinguished from the culture of liberalism, which is often anything but liberal.)[12] It seems almost inevitable that such an ethos must be incompatible with fierce, substantive, categorical and unquestioning belief, whether moral, political or religious. Liberality is a product of at least partial secularization and a symptom, if only distant, of incipient decadence. Fundamentalists of various hues are probably right on this point, and the future — if or when it arrives — of ignorant, vigorous, repressive barbarism will belong to them.

The ethos of liberality is barely separable from high culture as we nowadays think of it. It presupposes an ironic catholicity of outlook, a reluctance to be always claiming the moral high ground, and a general distrust of partisanship. All this leaves it ill-equipped to survive in a straight battle against the fervent, the unscrupulous and the intolerant. Liberality usually requires external protection and support. In the past this was often provided by some enlightened despot such as Frederick the Great. Nowadays it is typically the corporate rich who (though often admirably cultivated themselves) aspire to be socially accepted by the professional class, if we may so term them, of the cultivated.

The former, whom Nietzsche cruelly dubbed 'culture-Philistines', live in uneasy symbiosis with the latter, paying court to them despite their comparative poverty and political powerlessness. This last fact, by the way, which is a matter of common observation, ought finally to discredit the neo-Marxist theory of culture, according to which high culture is no more than the ideological expression and legitimation of the dominant socio-economic power or 'ruling class'. If this be doubted, consider the role of high culture — the real thing, not the official, state-sponsored substitute — as a focus of resistance in the latter days of Communism.

Roughly speaking, the main threat to the culture of liberality, and thus to intellectual manners, is whatever prizes certainty above truth or fails to recognize that *sub specie aeternitatis* some, perhaps most, truths are provisional. Newman thought that the liberal (or as he called them, the philosophical) virtues could be combined with Christianity, as well as (to their disadvantage) subsisting outside it. Nevertheless, it seems to me that religion for the most part *is* such a threat, unless we concede that theological liberalism and modernism are, in fact, authentically religious.[13] Political and moral enthusiasms are a similar threat. As noted earlier, those together with religion are the things which people really care about, so long, that is, as they do not care more for truth and the conditions of its flourishing as I have understood them. ('Truth' in religion does not mean what it does elsewhere. Religious 'truths' are matters of faith, and as such not subject to objective empirical confirmation. It would be more accurate to describe them as intuitions, experiences or perceptions which carry a subjective conviction equiponderous with what is normally called truth.)[14]

Fundamentalist religion and AIDS orthodoxy: two barriers to knowledge and civilized debate

To take religion at all seriously is necessarily to give it precedence over all other considerations, among which must be empirical inquiry and intellectual debate. Religion may enlist these so far as they reinforce it, but so far as they lead away from it they must obviously be discouraged. The whole point about religion is that to the believer it is precisely *not* (or in the convert's case no longer) an open question. To that extent it must inevitably conflict with the academic outlook, where nothing, apart, as I have already said, from the prevailing procedures and paradigms (and then only for so long as they survive unrevised), is ever wholly settled or immune from criticism. If religion really is the 'one thing necessary', then *odium theologicum* and everything ever done in its name, including the Inquisition, is more or less justified.[15] If people with the wrong ideas will go to Hell and we are to do our duty by them, they must obviously be protected from those wrong ideas, and others who already hold them must be persuaded, forcibly if necessary, to recant. (To be burnt to death for the good of one's soul is a bagatelle compared with burning throughout eternity.) With the stakes that high it must be idle to expect anything like a temperate discussion of the key issues.

It might be worth contrasting religious heresy with so-called intellectual or scientific heresies. Is it strictly speaking repressive or intolerant to exclude from the AIDS debate those, notably the Californian biologist Peter Duesberg, who deny that the syndrome has any connection with HIV? I should say it was not, but only so long as they have first been heard, and then found wanting. But even if they hadn't, no one ever proposed to burn Duesberg alive, despite the offence his theories caused, in particular to the 'safe sex' and 'heterosexual AIDS' lobbies. The opposite of the Inquisition's approach is not to accept everything that clamours to be heard; it is merely to admit to academic and intellectual debate everything, no matter how superficially outlandish, that shows itself prepared to abide by the normal rules and decencies. But to be admitted is to be guaranteed merely a hearing. The true enthusiast will usually settle for nothing less than acceptance, and complain of 'repression', 'discrimination' and the like when he does not get it.[16]

The AIDS controversy, of course, has long left behind both science and common sense, to say nothing of decency. It is so saturated with political and moral passions that almost nothing can be said about AIDS without raising somebody's hackles.[17] Duesberg's real notoriety derives not from his theory (which is subject to scientific criticism and debate like any other), but from its consequences, to the effect that if he is right, enormous efforts and resources have been expended, as hopes have been pinned, on a mare's nest. Add to this his unflattering observations on the homosexual lifestyle (to the effect that it is not promiscuous sodomy which has wrecked homosexuals' immune systems, but rather the drugs they take to facilitate it) and no one should be surprised at his rough ride, which is, indeed, the product of a modern, political *odium theologicum*. He simply cannot be allowed to be right. Fortunately for those with interests in the matter, it does indeed seem, independently, that he is not.

Thinkers such as Eric Voegelin and Norman Cohn have often observed that the violently illiberal political and moral enthusiasms of our time are the product of homeless religious impulses. Communism and Nazism, at least for the present, have run their course, and the baton (or should we say nightstick?) of fanaticism has passed to American left-liberal extremists of the 'politically correct' stripe, who as everyone knows are now wielding it vigorously.

The threat of tyranny to academic manners: collectivism and multiculturalism threaten pursuit of academic knowledge

It is scarcely necessary to illustrate how the older totalitarian doctrines corrupted intellectual life. Not only was 'communist' for decades almost a synonym for 'intellectual' in Britain, France and America, but in the early 1930s, to their eternal disgrace, no section of German society was more National Socialist than the (still autonomous) universities. Wholly indifferent to individuals, Nazis and Communists were dismissive of 'rights' generally, and naturally enough, since 'rights', if acknowledged, would have been a major obstacle to their designs. They were not averse, however, to legitimating their designs by invoking supposed *collective* rights: those of the nation, the master race, the proletariat or whatever. The point is simply that rights of this metaphysical kind, whether individual or collective, are absolute and irresistible, and can be made to justify virtually anything.

The politically correct in America have not been slow to understand this. For, in miscalled 'liberal' eyes, almost any oppressiveness or intrusiveness may be countenanced in the name of either 'individual' or 'minority' rights. For the purposes of this strategy women, being allegedly oppressed, are accorded 'minority' status despite actually being a majority. (Of course, no rights can be claimed on behalf of any *non*-'oppressed' majority, minority, or individual.) All kinds of follies, some of them quite sinister, have been perpetrated in American universities in the name of the imputed 'sensitivities' and 'rights to equal consideration' of supposedly disfavoured groups. Whole academic pseudo-subjects have been built around what are at best disputable, and at worst barely examined, contentions.

'Women's Studies', for example, is by no stretch of the imagination anything like an academic discipline. (It has now been renamed 'Gender Studies' to make it look like one. But nothing with the suffix 'Studies' will ever look like one.) By its own admission, and indeed proud boast, it is nothing less than the academic arm of feminism, which would be a serious criticism of it even if feminism were true (as some small part of it probably is). For no genuine academic discipline is, or can be, an 'arm' of anything. The academy's business is to ask and if possible answer questions, not to beg them, least of all to do so in favour of any extraneous cause or interest.

To beg such questions is to pre-empt the truth, to lay claim to it in advance of any impartial inquiry, and thus to destroy the very idea of it, to reduce it to a mere rhetorical stratagem. It is astonishing, but feminists, post-structuralists and others actually claim to be doing just those things. All these 'isms' form vague, shifting alliances, if only through their common opposition to the 'dominant discourse' of rationality. Among all their copious outpourings I cannot recall ever having registered a serious recognition on the author's part that he or she is caught in the old Sceptic's Paradox, to the effect that once one dismisses or relativizes the notions of objectivity, evidence and the 'truth' to which they lead, one thereby strips one's own case of any claim to credibility. To assert that there is no such thing as truth must mean, if it means anything at all (which is doubtful) that neither Marxism, nor feminism, nor 'theory', whatever else they may be, can be anything so vulgar as true.[18]

If there is no truth, or if 'truth' is socially or sexually conditioned (which amounts to the same as there being none), the very statement to that effect can be nothing more than ideology, and we thus have no reason, other than inclination, to accept it. *Ergo*, discussion is pointless, and force alone rules. This means that we can equally dismiss academic manners and all possibility of civilized discourse. And indeed this is just what is happening, as humanities departments splinter into ghetto-like factions united only by mutual distrust.

All this scepticism, curiously, is merely a convoluted version of the craving for certainty mentioned earlier. Here it takes the form of the assertion that the only truth, or certainty, is that there is no truth, only power. (Post-modernists might sidestep that conclusion by adding that there is no certainty either.) We are back, potentially, with *odium theologicum*, a passion that, in its original religious form, has been absent from mainstream Western culture for more than three centuries. In its other, mostly political atavars, unfortunately, it is still with us.

Personal attacks and their lack of concern for non-partisan, objective truth: the cases of Milton and Marx

One might mention a few historical examples. The first is ambiguous as between religion and politics, at a time when they were barely distinguishable. It is the controversy between Milton and Salmasius over the latter's *Defensio Regis*, a defence of monarchy and Charles I commissioned by the exiled Charles II. This is amusingly recounted in Johnson's 'Life of Milton' (*Lives of the Poets*, vol 1), where Johnson has already referred to Milton's 'puritanical savageness of manners'. Neither contender scrupled to ridicule the other's misfortunes: Salmasius's unhappy marriage, Milton's blindness. Such things seem to have been perfectly normal then, though today few polemicists would stoop to them. (That is one respect in which we can point to a definite improvement.)

Modern times are less entertaining. Once launched on his later career, Marx, though formerly a doctoral student, abandoned academic manners even where they most counted, in intellectual and philosophical matters. His polemics against Vogt, Proudhon and others are of such extraordinary violence, very often *ad hominem*, as to make it obvious that whatever is at stake, it cannot be truth. According to Edmund Wilson, Leopold Schwarzschild and others, Marx could not conduct a discussion without eventually shouting his opponents down. (Indeed, like Freud, he could barely believe in their good faith.) Since many were self-educated working men, he would often pull educational rank. 'For Marx', says Kenneth Minogue, 'to abandon a doctrine is to bleed.'[19] Marx paid heavily (and so, later, did the world) for his dogmatism and refusal to submit to criticism, in short for his self-imposed academic isolation. As a piece of economic theory *Capital* was already half a century or more out of date when it appeared, and (it seems to me) is also a clumsy, inelegant, ill-formed piece of thinking, besides being plainly wrong.[20]

Dogma and political strategies incompatible with academic discourse

Marx's intellectual passion was real. But Lenin's was synthetic, calculated and cynical. His polemic against idealist philosophy in the Russian Social Democratic Party, *Materialism and Empirio-Criticism*, suggests that he was wholly indifferent to anything resembling truth. This work is destitute of intellectual merit, being marked by astonishing philosophical crudity and (apparent) ignorance. But Lenin was an intelligent man. He was also without vanity in the normal sense, which would have held most writers back from publishing such a book. Most likely Lenin knew that what he was saying was neither true nor philosophically cogent. His evident object was strategic: to lay down a rigid line of dogma on disputed matters, so that the movement's energy should henceforth not be dissipated in irrelevant and politically fruitless academic squabbles, but concentrated instead on the task in hand, namely revolution. The latter is a matter not of theory, let alone of truth, but of practice, to which theory is at best instrumental.

The various political and religious threats to academic and intellectual discourse I have looked at all stem from an exclusively *practical* approach to life, to which all other considerations must perforce give place.[21] 'Philosophers hitherto have only interpreted the world,' wrote the young Marx brazenly; 'the point, however, is to change it.' The habitual cast of Lenin's mind is revealed by the title of his famous pamphlet 'What Is To Be Done?' (meant ironically to echo the elderly moralist Tolstoy). And history is full of religious fulminations against the 'pride of the intellect', curiosity, which ever since Eden has seduced man away from the only true path, that of obedience and its reward, a paradigm of the life of practice.

We should concede at least some priority to practical concerns. Without a surplus, which somebody must labour to produce, there can be no culture at all, and it ill beseems academics and intellectuals to forget that without others to carry on the everyday work and organization of the world they themselves would not exist. But that is different from requiring them to carry on the world's work in another guise, or to deny that any other kind of activity is possible. On this view everything but practice is ideology, being not merely supported by practice (which is true enough) but actively determined by it (which is not).

Civilized societies require free and ordered inquiry: deference and manners are essential to that search for truth

Practical considerations are not the only ones in a civilized society. For what makes it civilized is its ability to sustain so much that is both centrally human and practically useless. Vocational studies are both valid and useful, but the academic enterprise is corrupted when (as currently) they are implicitly being seen by governments as the paradigm of all intellectual endeavour. Somewhere in a civilized society there must always be thought for its own sake, if only because every ultimate value — art, love, friendship — similarly exists in and for itself, as production and the world's work do not.

Marxists, Gramscians, feminists, *et al*, whom we may take as an extreme type of the practice-oriented or activist mentality (another is the utilitarian), will presumably not deny that such ultimate ends or values are the real *telos* of human life. What they will deny is that they are realizable under current conditions. I do not know the radical line on love and friendship. But concerning scholarship, academic inquiry and liberal intellect generally, the line is clear, to the effect that they are not autonomous, but have the function of reinforcing and legitimating the existing social order and its structures of power.

This criticism is not as damaging and final as its proponents evidently suppose. First, a thing may have an undesigned function. It can exist in its own right, yet be simultaneously a meaningful or even useful part of some larger system to whose purposes it falls part and into which it fits. (Compare ecology.) If liberal culture should chance to underpin liberal society, that is not to say that its integrity or freedom is thereby compromised.

Far from it, in fact, for liberal or 'high' culture, above all others, is free to choose what social order it will support. Liberal culture was latterly an important centre of resistance to the 'existing social order' in Communist Europe, a fact which (as I have earlier noted) is sufficient to disprove the radical contention that liberal ideology merely justifies established power. And so far from being slavishly 'determined' by the societies in which it most flourishes, liberal culture is quick to point out their deficiencies. This, indeed, is a most valuable aspect of its 'function', making those societies largely self-correcting, and thus only the more deserving of its support.

Finally, what could be more natural than for liberal culture to support the political set-up most sympathetic to it? If, as Aristotle claims, liberal culture or something like it is the *telos* of the existing productive system (and not, as Marxists would say, only of some future, barely imaginable communist equivalent), then there will be nothing wrong with its 'legitimating' the liberal political order which sustains it, for that will amount to a perfectly valid justification. The complaint will be not so much false as trivial. If liberal culture (and indeed, the popular culture of a liberal society also) is free to confer legitimacy where it will, then whatever social order it declares legitimate must be so.

A culture which cares for truth will regard as legitimate whatever social order is best able to protect the truth and least inclined to maintain itself by lies. To respect the truth is to respect all who serve it, to see oneself as a member of a community of truth-seekers. The proud deference and self-effacement which that demands may very well be regarded as a kind of manners, and a kind, moreover, which should not inhibit even the most reticent from coming forward to defend the cause of truth in case of need.

9

Keeping Your Distance

Manners in the Surgery

Bruce Charlton

The essential unit of medical practice is the occasion when, in the intimacy of the consulting room or sick room, a person who is ill, or believes himself to be ill, seeks the advice of a doctor whom he trusts. This is a consultation and all else in the practice of medicine derives from it.

Sir James Spence ,The Purpose and Practice of Medicine

Professional manners essential for respect in personal encounters

Manners are the norms of society which provide rules for social intercourse, and useful manners will contribute to good communication and the ability of people to live together: they are the overt manifestation of respect for others. Manners will reflect the beliefs and values of society, and encompass figures of speech, modes of dress, and ways of behaving — different manners being appropriate to different situations. We are here concerned with manners in the context of professional practice.

Manners lie at the heart of good professional practice because professional practice is characterized by a personal relationship: a consultation. Yet all is not well. Bad manners on the part of doctors are a common cause of formal complaints. And doctors also complain (amongst themselves, at least) about increasing numbers of rude, inappropriately demanding and ungrateful patients. In this respect medicine seems to reflect a general decline in manners which affect professionals and public alike.

If not a decline, there has been a considerable change in manners over recent decades. This could be characterized as a shift away from 'formal' manners and towards 'friendly' manners. Formal manners tend to be clear, fixed, uniform, publicly agreed and emotionally reserved; and to express in ceremonial form the idea of *respect*. By contrast, friendly manners are fluid, pluralistic, individually negotiated according to circumstances; and express the idea of *affection*.

This shift in manners can be tracked in the style of advertisements, which so often provide a barometer of social attitudes. Advertisers of personal services (banks, fast food retailers, car repair workshops, etc) which in the past would have attempted to project an image of dependability, solidity and respectful politeness, now tend to emphasize a friendly welcome by likeable staff — even in situations where a more formal relationship might seem more appropriate. Such an expectation or idealization of friendly manners presents problems when mutual respect is necessary to the proper functioning of a relationship.

Since professionals represent their clients' interests, their manners should reflect the ethics of that relationship

Professional practice is a complex social role, and professionals are not simply in the business of providing 'expertise'. There is also a need for trust because the professional must act in the client's interests. A client's interests cannot be fully represented if there is no personal relationship. Because there is a relationship of a special kind, much of the special value of the professional practice is inherent in its manner. The therapeutic benefits of good manners in medicine is only an extreme example of the fact that form cannot be disassociated from content in a professional relationship.

Yet manners are frequently regarded as distinctly 'peripheral' in importance, and neglected in favour of quantifiable or material goals relating to expertise and efficiency. This is a result of instrumental modes of reasoning which regard the consultation as a means towards ends other than the client's best interest.

The professions should therefore have a particular concern for manners. But there is a problem. Manners are a part of larger society and the degraded or, at best, 'friendly' quality of common, expected public manners in a liberal, pluralistic society is inadequate for professional practice. In such circumstances, the professions must create and sustain their own codes of manners and ensure that the public understands them in order to enable reliable communication. Historically, manners have been entwined with ethical codes, and it seems reasonable to expect that better than usual manners should be part of professional practice, just as we expect a higher than usual standard of ethics from professionals in relation to their work.

If we agree that the 'essential unit of medical practice' is the consultation, where the client seeks the advice of a professional whom he trusts, then a personal encounter is at the root of clinical medicine. A similar argument applies *mutatis mutandis* to other professional relationships. The circumstances surrounding the consultation and the manner of that consultation are seen to be of great importance.

It is therefore convenient to discuss manners in a professional context by analyzing the consultation in a step by step fashion.

The environment should be suitable for the consultation

The doctor's office should be designed so that the consultation may proceed as smoothly as possible, without disturbance or intrusion of unwanted or irrelevant features. Broadly speaking, this will involve aiming at a quiet, comfortable and secluded environment; an environment which is pleasant for the client and which encourages a calm and collected frame of mind.

Naturally, there are always constraints of resources which mean that conditions will never be ideal. And it is a discourtesy for the doctor to decorate and equip the consultation rooms such that they fail to provide the privacy which is pre-requisite to that confidentiality without which a professional relationship cannot proceed.

If, for example, the office walls are decorated with health promotion posters designed to induce the patient to change his lifestyle, this is merely treating the client as part of a mass audience. Even if effective, such techniques are likely to induce anxiety and a set of preoccupations which may interfere with the consultation proper. If, as research suggests, such techniques are ineffective, then impersonal health promotion is bad manners to a patient who is seeking a consultation. Alternatively, if the walls are covered by 'in jokes' then this signals that the amusement of the staff has taken priority over the desires of clients.

Of course, such obligations are reciprocal; and it would be expected that the clients' demeanour and behaviour would be appropriate to the goals of the consultation, and contribute towards a calm and collected atmosphere.

First names unsuitable as a standard form of address

Part of the shift towards 'friendly' manners has been a decline in the traditional (distanced and respectful) professional medical manners. According to this view, doctor and patient are supposed to relate to each other as if they were bound by ties of affection rather than ties of responsibility. Such reasoning underlies the vast and bogus rhetoric of the 'caring professions'.

This view lies behind the use of first names among strangers — a desire to assume instant intimacy as a basis for the relationship. Although first-naming may be well-intentioned, when premature or insensitive it may be interpreted as disrespectful, especially by members of the older generation who make up the majority of patients as well as a substantial minority of doctors. Furthermore, first-naming may be done in a manipulative fashion (it is notable that some of the most intrusive first-namers are salesmen).

The maintenance of a habit of formal address as the norm also allows a shift to the use of first names as a significant step in a professional relationship when a more intense and personal element is appropriate. For instance, in the long-term management of a terminally ill patient, the doctor and patient may choose to call each other by first names at a certain point. This signals that the relationship has moved towards a closer, more 'supportive' form. This places greater demands upon both parties, and cannot be taken as the norm or assumed to be universally applicable; but such mutual understanding nevertheless may form a high water mark for the professional relationship.

The manners of appearance: the importance of formal clothing

There has also been a shift in dress codes in recent decades: a decline in uniforms and other conventional forms of dress, and the adoption of a variety of more casual clothes. Dress is increasingly seen as a public expression of individual personality, or is used to signal allegiance to particular ideological or social groupings. But a potential hazard lies in the half-considered view that formal dress in doctors is somehow repressive; while smart dress in patients is servile and indicative of inferiority in status.

Formality of dress then becomes perceived negatively, as a political statement. This is unhelpful at best and harmful at worst; indeed, imposed informality is usually discriminatory against the shy and unconfident who are left without guidance about how to behave.

But considerations of dress ought to be in the background because such considerations are, at best, irrelevant to the purpose of a professional relationship. Dress may become actively ill-mannered when either the doctor or the patient is, implicitly, engaged in thrusting their political stance or disdain for established status into the foreground or a situation with other goals. The prominent display of lapel badges indicative of support for political or pressure groups is an egregious example of this sort of discourtesy. There is much to be said in favour of standard uniforms and conventional clothes when this allows the question of dress to be ignored in favour of more important matters.

Intimacy between doctors and patients must not impinge on professional distance and judgement

Professional respect, emotional distance, and formal good manners may be an important safeguard against abuse. They enable both professional and client to adopt a *role* which is specific to the relationship, and which has boundaries of a mutually understood nature. This is vital to medicine where a high degree of personal disclosure or even actual physical contact may be necessary.

Although a degree of intimacy is essential, the doctor's role is of course circumscribed, and he does not have the authority to dictate the patient's whole life, nor to ask questions irrelevant to health, nor to erode the patient's autonomous right to make decisions. The consultation ought to be bounded in this way, and this demarcation may be unselfconsciously and harmoniously achieved by a distinctive manner which signals that a particular kind of specifically professional relationship is underway.

Formal manners may also help prevent the necessary intimacy of a medical consultation from arousing powerful (and often damaging) emotional or sexual responses. Participants are continually reminded, through the maintenance of formal distance, that what is afoot is a special kind of relationship, not to be mixed up with a relationship based upon personal affection. It is noticeable that sexual contact seems to be most common in those branches of the health care professions (or *soi disant* professions) where the scope for professional responsibility is widest and where boundaries are least clear: namely psychotherapy and counselling.

Because 'friendly manners' are so close to 'manners between friends', indeed informal manners are attempting to simulate the spontaneity and flexibility of friendship, the confusion between the two may exert a damaging effect upon friendship. When formal manners are the norm, the demarcation of friendship is easily accomplished by the shift to a different form of address. In the absence of such discrimination, doctors and patients are alike confronted with a large grey area of uncertainty.

Bureaucracy undermining trust in professional relations

Charters have been introduced into professional relationships in the United Kingdom at the same time as moves to 'encourage' customers to lodge formal complaints against professionals. Examples are the 'patient's charter' and the 'citizen's charter' — more are being considered. Each takes the form of a series of explicit rights or standards which the client is entitled to expect from 'public services'.

The culture of charters and complaints seems to be a crude attempt to inject elements of formality and responsibility into a professional context of increasing informality. The consultation, instead of being a seamless process of distanced and respectful good manners, becomes divided into parts characterized by a simulation of informal friendship and parts dictated by bureaucratic regulation imposed externally. So the doctor might break off from 'friendly' conversation to read the patient a list of his 'rights' (guaranteed by a third party) then ask him to sign at the bottom that this procedure has been done according to the rules. The form is filed and copies are kept by all parties.

Insofar as the professional relationship conforms to the ideal of a relationship based on trust, the introduction of quasi-legal and explicit standards and procedures for formal complaints will have a damaging effect. Standards and complaints are imposed and monitored externally. A third party is put in a position of authority over the consultation, which is thereby diminished. The process of implementing standards will introduce a new layer of (presumably) expensive and (probably) unwieldy bureaucracy. But more importantly, a third party who was not present at the consultation will be able to make only the crudest of judgements about its content, amounting merely to the apportionment of 'blame'. In a professional context, complaints will inevitably, and justifiably, be interpreted as evidence of failure, and the frequent exhortations to regard complaints in a constructive fashion are misguided and futile.

Indeed, the notion of a society where manners (or a legalistic simulation of manners) are imposed and monitored by government, is both absurd and ill conceived. If successful, the result would be the elimination from our lives of that mutuality which is one of the most valued aspects of culture. The replacement of implicit trust by explicit contract and legal protocol would be an attack on civil society of the kind we associate with totalitarian regimes.

Professional manners fundamental to professional endeavour

It is striking how similar the ideals of medical manners and practice are between the UK and the USA; despite the two countries having radically different systems of health service organizations and funding. This implies that the ideals of behaviour may transcend the nature of economic arrangements. Broadly the same standards of behaviour are expected of doctors whatever their country, in all specialities, whether they be salaried or paid by item of service, whether there be a socialized system of medicine, insurance payers or private contracts, whether the doctor is an employee or an independent contractor.

It therefore seems mistaken to interpret manners, as many do, as merely a secondary manifestation of economic 'reality', derivative of the structures of society in general and health care in particular. It would be more true to say that economics and the structures necessary to civil society are possible only in societies which are held together by manners among other things. Professional manners are not epiphenomena, but are fundamental to professional endeavour.

Professional relationships rely on trust which depends on a distinctive role

A good professional relationship is characterized by trust, and if the public are to be able to recognize and trust professionals, a distinctive manner is appropriate. The manner best suited to professional activities is, I would argue, one characterized by respectful distance and formal manners. There are exceptions to this general rule, and considerable room for individual adjustment; but however trust is achieved it remains the vital prerequisite to the professional relationship, and cannot be replaced by regulations. Recent attempts to 'reform' the professions are often indicative of a basic distrust of the nature of the professional-client relationship, and seem driven by a desire to abolish professions and replace them with another kind of relationship which is simpler, cheaper and easier to regulate.

Reforms which aim to replace professionals typically fail, because the professional relationship represents a response to powerful public demand for services to be provided by an agent whom they can trust. In the end, hostile reforms succeed only in weakening the professional *ethos*, and encouraging an atmosphere of cynicism on both sides; something which can only be bad for the public. All available alternatives to professions are likely to prove more complex, more expensive, less flexible and, finally, incapable of fulfilling their function. It seems that there is no realistic alternative but to trust professionals. Reforms must therefore be directed at ensuring that a high standard of professional ethics is inculcated and sustained. This implies a strong system of self-regulation.

Manners need to be put back to a place of prominence in education and clinical practice. Although the professions cannot altogether be cut off from general trends, medicine must set its own house in order when changes in public manners strike at the heart of the consultation. The sanction for failing to achieve appropriate manners would be declining public trust and support, and a shift of allegiance (and resources) away from those individuals and groups whose practice fails to incorporate those manners the public expect, and for which they pay.

The paradox of a professional relationship is that the professional offers a personal service but in an impersonal context: a service available to every client without regard to personal likes and dislikes between the parties. Indeed, circumstances will often dictate that the doctor and patient may *not* like each other, and may differ profoundly in their attitudes to life. Yet professional manners should be such that any personal incompatibilities will not interfere with the professional relationship. The availability of a code of behaviour based upon the formalized embodiment of respect is stronger, more appropriate, convenient and acceptable than an informal code based upon an assumption of universal and undiscriminating personal affection.

> Fortunately, the good life is not a matter of economics. It is a matter of manners, of ethics and of moral philosophy, with charity as its safest guide for most of us.
>
> Sir James Spence, *The Purpose and Practice of Medicine*

Acknowledgements are due to Professor James McCormick and Dr Gillian Rye

10

Running a Respectable Household

Habits of the Home and Social Order

Michael D Aeschliman

Traditional values undermined by pluralism of modern liberal society

> *Part of the trouble stems from the fact that sociology is the documentation of original sin by those who believe in original virtue.*
>
> David Martin[1]

Over 20 years have elapsed since this assertion by the sociologist David Martin, and in the intervening period the belief in 'original virtue' has finally become so incredible as to be untenable. *Both* parties within our dominant liberalism — Libertarians or 'Manchester Liberals' and Leftists or 'Welfare-State Liberals' — have begun to recognize, deplore, and really worry about the anarchic disintegration of the social texture of civilized life in our time.[2] The true conservative ought to be forgiven for saying that he and his tradition had said it first and repeatedly but were systematically ignored or excluded from consideration. First and forgotten.[3] The conservatives — Burke, de Maistre, Newman, Kierkegaard, Dostoevsky, and their modern successors and followers — told the truth and depicted the destructive future too soon: voices crying warning in the wilderness of optimistic illusions, they were mocked, impugned, or neglected. And now, perhaps, it is too late; *sero sapiunt*.

Thus of modern liberalism generally the critic Robert Pattison, himself a liberal, tells us that 'The modern world constructed by liberalism is as [John Henry] Newman foresaw a network of inferences without a beginning'. This 'anti-foundationalism' is a point of pride with many contemporary thinkers, such as Richard Rorty, but its moral consequences are at best anomalous and troubling, and perhaps, finally, lethal to personal decency and social order. 'The modern', Pattison writes, 'believes everything and nothing. He adopts a philosophy monthly or yearly'.[4] There are, of course, euphemisms for this state of affairs — mobility, perspectivalism, individualism, liberation — but it is very bad news for both the idea and the possibility of moral order, 'civilization', or any *res publica*. Some 'liberations', as Goethe long ago noted,[5] are pernicious or even fatal: liberation from the 'common sense' of the religious Natural-Law moral tradition arguably being the most obvious one. It may be tolerable for a minority elite of educated intellectuals to repose upon what Newman called 'the broad bosom of skepticism', but can a *society* survive long on such 'beliefs'?[6]

The family in particular vulnerable to erosion

Apparently families cannot, and a vast and growing sociological literature attests both to the erosion of the contemporary family and to the disastrous effects of the erosion on society.[7] The Oxford sociologist A H Halsey said in 1991 that he 'shuddered for the next generation of children brought up in single-parent families', which are increasing at the rate of 40,000 a year in Britain alone, with illegitimacy rates there now as high or higher than in the USA.[8] Data from the US are even more troubling, and a recent popular treatment of the issue makes the claim that there is a 'worldwide crisis in parenting' and a 'general breakdown in parental morale', leading to a 'betrayal of childhood...on a world-wide scale'.[9]

It is to some extent appropriate to blame this development on permissive child-rearing, 1960s radicalism, the 'entertainment culture' of consumer hedonism, and the anarchic capitalism that is implicated in all three, as thoughtful and earnest critics such as Daniel Bell, Christopher Lasch, and Neil Postman have done.[10] 'Liberations' from constraint such as contraception, abortion, de-stigmatized homosexualism, co-habitation, divorce, and illegitimacy have changed the nature of social relations with unprecedented rapidity and thoroughness within the last two generations in the cosmopolitan 'first world' made possible — even inescapable — by the global communications and transportation revolutions.[11] With CNN and MTV, there are no significant 'backwaters of conservatism', to speak of, left.

It is now a sociological commonplace, but a valuable one, that modern societies are suffering an extended and deepening 'crisis of legitimacy', a series of intra-national and transnational 'culture wars' over the grounds, if any, of authority, and attendant struggles for cultural power.[12] Robert Nisbet has written of our era as *The Twilight of Authority*, and he does not, like so many 'progressive' intellectuals of the last 250 years, welcome this development.[13] Authority, a standard, simple, brief definition has it, is 'the untested acceptance of another's judgment',[14] and it is fair to assert that its roots, humanly speaking, are in the deference of infants and children to their parents. The family is thus not only the school of virtue and citizenship, civilizing and socializing the egocentric and transgressive impulses of the infant, the child, and the adolescent on the way to understanding and developing 'maturity' and 'personhood'; it is the prime school of reality formation itself.[15] Without its maintenance and transmission of rational and moral common sense, largely consisting of decent, proverbial 'prejudices' that are prior to reason and criticism, specifically *human*, as opposed to *animal*, life is not possible.[16]

Human existence rooted in habits, morals, and manners learnt in the family

Specifically *human* life is not, initially, founded or rooted in reason and criticism but in manners and habits learned by imitating authoritative 'others' — first and foremost parents. 'Manners are minor morals', but minor only in the sense of being incessantly required in contexts and ways that usually do not attract conscious notice because they are so small and numerous. Patterns of deference toward the elderly and guests, and courtesy toward service personnel, may or may not be reinforced outside the home in the culture at large, but they are first legitimated within the family — they are 'taken on faith'. Self-discipline; emotional balance; an aversion to profanity and obscenity; truth-telling; public reticence about 'private' affairs; and an understanding of degrees of intimacy: all are first learned and credited in the family — or nowhere at all. They are fences, screens, or bulwarks against demoralization and emotional anarchy, against the age-old human horror of lassitude and chaos. As an old adage has it:

> Keep order in space
> And order in time,
> For disorder is chaos
> And chaos is crime.

Habits of human orderliness, politeness, and dignity — polishing shoes, making beds, gardening, setting tables, writing letters — can keep persons humanly alive through periods of depression and crisis. Decent, ingrained manners and habits can solve or mitigate big problems, or tame them so that they are tolerable. Numerous novels of the last 250 years display the reality of these 'humanizing' traditions. It was a profound comment of Lionel Trilling, however, that the 'failure to conceive the actuality of the life of common routine' — to *appreciate* it — 'is typical of modern literature since, say, Tolstoy', who died in 1910.[17]

Dominance of individualism in much nineteenth-century American literature and its rejection of moral judgment

The literature of the American South was the greatest of American literatures in the period 1920-1960 and part of its greatness is to be found in its depiction of a world in which religion and the family are still constitutive of social reality, and in which manners are still vividly important.[18] But the innovative, anarchic individualism promoted in the American North in the nineteenth century was, alas, finally to shape and inspire the direction of the 'national' literary, artistic, and intellectual culture that governs us today. Emerson, Thoreau, and especially Whitman denied the primacy of tradition, creed, church, and family, in the interest of the liberated, 'imperial' self that could pride itself on being 'beyond' mere conventions such as 'bourgeois' or 'sectarian' ethics. Whitman understood, the scholar Quentin Anderson has argued, 'that a rejection of Christianity on behalf of an emotional egalitarianism would have to begin with a rejection of the idea that the self was internally structured by conscience'.[19] Augmented by a century of social Darwinism, this Nietzschean aestheticism — often explicitly homosexual — is now our dominant sensibility, with the sado-masochistic photographs of the homosexual Mapplethorpe a good example. Nietzsche's aristocratic contempt for the still earnest, though post-Protestant moralism of George Eliot has been articulated and asserted against normative morality and traditional institutions such as the family by an ever-growing chorus of aesthetes and sexual liberationists. Nor is this only an American development. Thus André Gide wrote with fastidious aesthetic and avant-garde scorn: 'You remind me of certain Englishmen; the more their minds are emancipated, the more they cling to morality'.[20]

'Clinging to morality' is bad taste, infantile fetishism, emotional timidity, or evidence of 'an authoritarian personality', to the advanced intellectual consensus of our academy and media today. The 'traditional' family is a sexist prison inflicting excessive, unique loyalties and forms of guilt and indebtedness, frequently in alliance with oppressive religious superstitions. As the controllers make clear in Aldous Huxley's *Brave New World*, monogamy and family are to the 'progressive' mind the very sources of illusion and neurosis:

> Family, monogamy, romance. Everywhere exclusiveness, a narrow channelling of impulse and energy...No wonder these poor pre-moderns were mad and wicked and miserable. Their world did not allow them to take things easily.[21]

And *Brave New World* is a mindless pornotopia as a result of the victory of the 'progressive' techno-bureaucratic and therapeutic elite over the 'superstitious' pre-moderns with their inhibitions and obsessions, their unique loves and loyalties, their Shakespeare, Cardinal Newman, and Dostoevsky.

Although deficiency of virtue is not new, it is now, as never before, considered unimportant

Of course one ought not to deny or ignore the fallibility of the family or promote any idea of a golden age within history from which the contemporary world has fallen away; even with the highest, finest, and apparently healthiest cultural traditions human beings in every age have nevertheless found ample scope for folly, vice, sin, and destructiveness. But in our time the very *ideas* of normative moral belief, language, and behaviour in the West have suffered unprecedented erosion. In the early twentieth century Charles Péguy was prophetic in insisting that the real heroes of the late twentieth century would thus be the parents of decent families.[22]

Though long considered a man of the Left, the distinguished American social historian Eugene Genovese has recently written almost apocalyptically about this erosion. American liberals, he writes, 'have mounted a ferocious assault on the two-parent family, the social norm of heterosexuality, parental authority, and anything that smacks of serious religious commitment', and he deplores the Democratic 'party's surrender to radical feminists, gay liberationists, and thinly disguised nihilists who are assaulting what remains of family structure'.[23]

Against the cosmopolitan insouciance of Manchester Liberalism and the brutal rhetoric of Marxist revolutionism, with their respective, comforting abstractions and teleologies, great pens were lifted in the nineteenth century in defence and depiction of the family as the main bulwark against social chaos and the reign of the wolf. However fateful, limiting, and sometimes tragically oppressive the family could be, in Walter Scott, Jane Austen, Dickens, Manzoni, Hawthorne and Tolstoy it is, with the religion that legitimates it, the only mitigation of the anxieties, manias, and rapacities to which the human person is prone. Nevertheless, under the influence of the growing secularization of the nineteenth century, a pervasive desacralization and disorientation of family and social life were set in motion which have reached great speed and momentum in our own time. The great American Southern writers of the period 1920-1960 were the moral successors of the great Victorians. In the essays, poems, stories and novels of Andrew Lytle, Allen Tate, William Faulkner, James Agee, and Flannery O'Connor, in different but related ways, we may see the residual momentum of a civilization being consciously defended and renewed. The 'twelve Southerners' who wrote the manifesto *I'll Take My Stand* in 1930 created one of the great documents of American civilization in our century, consciously attempting both a renewal and transmission of the same values of conservation, small scale, religion, localism and family that their English Distributist allies such as Chesterton were defending across the sea.[24] Both had a horror of the abstractions and gigantism promoted equally by Left collectivism and rapacious capitalism. No finer book on the clash of loyalties between traditional piety and the emergent, social Darwinist, amoral individualism has ever been written than Allen Tate's enduringly poignant Civil-War novel *The Fathers*, published in 1938.[25]

Cult of individualism has led to idea of the 'accidental' family

Nevertheless, these Southerners were ultimately — or at least temporarily — defeated by the glamorous culture and literature of anarchy, 'liberation', hedonism, and 'styles of radical will', starting with the 'Beat' poets and the 'Rock' musicians, rebels without a cause and sons who hated or rejected their fathers and the very idea of decent parental authority and 'adult' behaviour.[26] Although only Norman Mailer wrote a book called *Advertisements for Myself*, this title might be said to express the burgeoning artistic sensibility of the last 50 years, eventuating in 'the culture of Narcissism'. As so often was the case, it was Dostoevsky who had had an uncanny intuition in its early stages of this nihilistic development whose outcome in and beyond our own age is so ominous. 'One cannot deny that a way of life in Russia is disintegrating', he wrote in his *Diary of a Writer* in the 1870s; 'consequently, family life disintegrates as well'.[27] To describe one of its effects, he coined a phrase that is more and more accurate as a description of our own social landscape and configurations 125 years later — 'the accidental family'.[28]

He wrote:

> The accidental nature of today's Russian family consists in the loss among contemporary fathers of any common idea about their families — an idea common to all fathers that binds them together, an idea which they could believe and could teach their children to believe, passing on to them this faith for the rest of their lives.[29]

In light of sociological and historical researches such as Acquaviva's *The Decline of the Sacred in Industrial Society* and Owen Chadwick's *The Secularization of the European Mind in the 19th Century*, we may speak more analytically and precisely about these phenomena that Dostoevsky perceived and depicted. The family, Acquaviva writes,

> which for centuries was an eminently conservative agency with respect to the sacred, [has changed radically in our time, and by and large no longer] maintains and defends common traditions. For centuries before the modern age, [the family was] the focal centre of social life [and] kept the individual immune from external influence to a large extent.[30]

Moral leadership in the family has faded with the increasing tide of external influences

With the unprecedented invasiveness of modern technologies such as television, radio, tape decks, and even automobiles and telephones, the external influences — and attractions — have often overwhelmed and eliminated any unique family intimacies and bonds and trans-generational family loyalties and beliefs. Yet long before the technological revolution had moved into high gear in the 1960s, Dostoevsky had detected that the 'common idea' that the fathers of *his* day were losing or lacking was a philosophical-moral essence, a sense of the sacred and a framework of value that they 'could teach their children to believe'. The bond of the generations and the internal gravitational core of the sound, decent, traditional family — however embattled and wounded by contingency — was a narrative and a faith, trans-personal and inspiring. Dostoevsky asserted

> It is only a great faith of this kind that is capable of giving birth to *something beautiful* in the memories of children [and] a person must not leave childhood and go into life without the rudiments of something beautiful and positive.[31]

This lack of and need for an inspiring image, a moral narrative, a faith — however unspoken, inchoate, or semi-conscious — is at the root of the contemporary family 'problem'. The late Black Civil-Rights leader Ralph Abernathy suggested in his memoirs that Blacks in the segregated communities of Alabama in the 1930s, when he grew up there, had this vision, and that it enabled them to live amidst adversity and poverty, to build and maintain decent marriages, families, and communities, to shape and live out lives of dignity, and sometimes nobility. He was greeted with silence or scorn when he suggested that contemporary people — Black and White — had lost this habitual vision, and were the poorer for it.[32]

That the 'entertainment industry' in Hollywood and New York bears an immense responsibility for this degradation and degeneration seems indisputable, as the 'adversary culture' has its most powerful engine in this profitable factory of images, dialogue, lyrics, and rhythm whose stage and market are now the world. The imitative behaviour of children was once primarily modelled on parents, siblings, close friends, and regional or national heroes who bore the stamp of approval from constituted authority in the home, school, and church. Now a culture of blatantly transgressive individuals and images has replaced this pantheon of imitable models, and a capitalist 'culture' may thus liquidate the older sources and momentum of social sanity that made its peace, prosperity, and leisure possible in the first place.[33]

Culture of egalitarianism and self-indulgence fostered by outside influences can best be challenged by a revival of strong family morality

One of the most obvious symptoms and causes of the degeneration in mores is the decline of normative or 'bourgeois' manners, both inside and outside the family. As Goethe knew, manners have profound roots and implications.[34] 'Manners are minor morals.' The modern egalitarian style, for which America is now the model and the envy of the youth of the world, is profoundly anarchic and demoralizing in its effects and implications, effacing differences between degrees of intimacy, the private and the public, the informal and the formal, and all traditional hierarchies of value and discrimination.[35] The egalitarian style yearns for and encourages a thorough-going profanation of social relations, an evisceration and elimination of anything sacred, exalted, dignified, profound, or permanent. Even the liturgy and clergy of the Roman Catholic Church have been infected by it, in a vain and spurious attempt for relevance, immediacy, spontaneity, and 'sincerity'.

Despite this degradation of manners and mores, the battered family seems to be the only institution on the social landscape capable of salvaging and restoring civilization, or at least resisting and opposing its complete collapse. Despite the immense potency of the degrading cultural environment and images promoted and endlessly purveyed by the communications media — a potency irresistible by single families without a religious bulwark and background or heroic individual efforts — it is still conceivable and possible for such families *with* religious support and legitimation to oppose it; but it is a culture war that must be fought, within the limits of law and decency, against *all* the forms of liberalism, which have effectively both brought about the degradation and dominated and blighted the discussion of social questions for so long.

Whether, in spite of a long mutual history of sectarian suspicion and antipathy, traditional, orthodox Protestants, Catholics, and Jews can find their way to an effective alliance, based on revelation and some version of Natural Law, an alliance against liberals both within and beyond their faith communities, may well determine whether the family in any historically recognizable form can be renewed as an antidote to social atomism and decomposition and moral anarchy.[36]

11

Why Do It?
Because That's What *We* Do

Manners in the Ruins of Community

H Tristram Engelhardt, Jr

Relationship of morals and manners in the ordered society

Morals and good manners are not the same. Yet they are not that different. Both are concerned with values and behaviour. Both good manners and morals are challenged by our failure to share (or our recognition that we no longer share) a common understanding of life's meaning or the character of proper behaviour. In their particularity, our traditional canons of good manners are a further sign of our divisions. Our manners are eurocentric (ie, ours are the manners of Europeans). Rather than this being a point in favour of manners (did not Europe fashion our contemporary world culture?), this particularity is perceived by many as discrediting our traditional elements of courtesy. Though good manners should be an expression of mutual respect and social solidarity, our manners are often received as anti-manners. Rather than sustaining social solidarity, they disclose fundamental disagreements regarding our cultural identity and our values.

Against this background, what can one make of good manners? How can one sustain good manners if one can identify them? This chapter will explore the nature of manners and their bond to intact moral traditions. A distinction will be drawn between the manners that bind those joined in a thick understanding of proper conduct (here referred to as friends, those with whom one has a thick binding of commitment in culture and manners) and those that foster collaboration with strangers. Finally, some closing reflections will be advanced regarding the future of manners in an age when traditions are in disarray and decay.

Manners, values and social bonds in civil society

Manners are embedded in a complex social fabric richly framed with values and directed towards particular visions of human flourishing. Manners express a particular set of values; endorse particular exemplars of proper deportment; are sustained by and reinforce a particular social nexus; while often, in addition, affirming a particular metaphysics, a particular understanding of the deep structure of reality, as well as its meaning. Manners have an axiological dimension. They guide deportment. They are integral to particular social structures. They can intimate truths. As scientific theories distinguish between noise and information, good manners do so by identifying considerate and inconsiderate conduct out of a universe of behaviour, much of which is inconsiderate. Good manners interpret and transform social reality. They provide social orientation. They direct personal energies and guide behaviour.

The term manners is richly ambiguous. It identifies a number of social phenomena associated through various family resemblances. 'Manners' has connections with the Latin *manuarius*, belonging to the hand, itself a term derived from *manus*. This derivation suggests that manners are ways of getting things in hand, of rendering them manageable, tractable. Manners provide ways of mastering a situation through showing respect towards others, supporting common values and endorsing social solidarity. The term has meanings that range from a form of expression to a customary mode of acting, including usage, form, and fashion. Manners identify as well the subject of morality itself. Manners concern the ways in which individuals should behave, deport themselves, and conduct themselves with others. As such, manners are not just modes of behaviour, but properly good manners, polished courtesy, canons of civility. In this chapter, the focus is on manners as polite behaviour. Manners are that deportment indicative of good breeding expressed in appropriate forms of politeness and courtesy.

Manners, though not morals, are an important civilizing force

There are many values important to the good life, which are not in and of themselves moral values. Judgments regarding the sublimity of a scene in nature, the beauty of a painting, the excellence of a wine, all involve values, though not moral values. So, too, judgments regarding manners involve non-moral assessments of the excellence and grace of deportment. Manners also have moral significance. They are embedded in moral understandings. But their peculiar focus is on a non-moral sphere of values. The Romans' *humanissimus vir* was a man of excellence, who realized both intellectual virtues as well as refinement of taste, even when his pagan moral virtues may have been in decay. So, too, a lady or gentleman appropriately incarnates excellences of deportment, which are not only moral.

Manners can support both civility and morals even in the conduct of immoral actions. Manners like hypocrisy can pay a tribute to background moral understandings. For example, though one may very well condemn duelling as immoral, one can understand the good manners by which a gentleman should conduct a duel. Armies at war have ceased hostilities for a common Christmas celebration and shown courtesy and civility to each other without even considering how Christians ought appropriately to resolve disputes, or the comparative justice of the two sides in battle. Manners affirm framing traditions, moral commitments, and metaphysical understandings, even when individuals and groups fail to realize the moral virtues endorsed by those traditions and their morals. They provide minimal rules of considerate behaviour even when one is violating moral rules.

Community dependent on shared values which manners help to maintain

Good manners betoken a community, however thin. In a homogeneous culture united in common traditions and strong in its moral practices, there is no gulf between morals and manners. Where throne and altar are united in a coherent moral vision, proper deportment reflects a vision of how things ought to be, of how one should act, of how one should be moral, and of how one should show courtesy. But even within thick and coherent world views, there are contrasts between the rules of morality and courtesy. In Christendom, the contrast of morals and manners reflects the circumstance that morals have transcendent significance. Manners have at best instrumental, facilitatory, or local character. All should have good morals, the claims of morality are universal, and the content of morality is binding on all. Though moral understandings may be nurtured by particular communities with particular histories, their moral claims as moral claims are directed to all. Manners, on the other hand, are conventional and in their particularity local. The canons of courtesy in Japan are not those observed by the best families in the American South. Still, though manners may be conventional in character, when they are well-ordered, they support the underlying morality.

Manners and morals in intact moral communities

Manners tend to be set within larger moral concerns. Consider a contrast between morals and conventional courtesies in a highly traditional community: Orthodox Christianity. All Orthodox Christians are bound in a common morality, though manners differ, depending on whether one is Finnish or Japanese, Texan or Lebanese. There is nothing clearly wrong in the circumstance that Japanese tend to bow to each other as they stand in line for confession and that they rarely embrace each other, delivering a brace of kisses. The bowing appears not only innocent, but even praiseworthy as an expression of humility and respect. Still, what of their reticence to kiss in greeting? Perhaps, since the Apostles greeted each other with a kiss, so, too, should the Japanese. If Texans can learn such manners, why cannot the Japanese? Yet, the matter is not as essential as are the Commandments, the canons, and the teachings of ecumenical and regional councils. Still, there is something out of place in meeting Christians who simply exchange bows or handshakes, rather than a kiss.[1] As distant as are Ethiopia and Alaska, India and the Czech Republic, to be Orthodox is still to be orthodox. All should feel the same desire to return to the Fathers, to live in their vision, and to see things as they received manners from the Apostles. Christianity is a way of life that should as far as possible be maintained along with its received usages. If one meets as brothers, one should meet in a kiss.[2]

This very particular example illustrates how a world-wide community can be united in a common morality, yet divided in manners. It shows as well how a moral community can reshape manners. It brings into question a diversity of manners, a diversity of respectful greetings, leads to a re-examination of differences, and redirects them within a tradition towards a common moral vision. A tradition carries practices with it as well as the bases for revising practices. In this case, the mode of recognizing a brother in the Faith can be regarded as not merely a matter of convention, but as having moral significance. Manners and morality are bound together even where there is a disparity of customs and a diversity of manners. Because manners are embedded within the larger and more substantial context of a moral vision, manners can be obliged to express the background moral vision. Although manners are not as central to the good life as are good morals, they support the good life.

The term morals can identify behaviour essential to determining praiseworthiness and blameworthiness, worthiness of happiness and unworthiness of happiness. Manners, in contrast, concern behaviour important in determining social adeptness. A man can be of good heart but innocently thoughtless, vulgar of expression, and lacking in social graces. He can be of good morals but bad manners. He can be of good morals but not understand the canons of courtesy. Still, there is an obligation to have good manners so as appropriately to discharge obligations (eg, adequately to express thanks) and to show respect. Insofar as courtesy supports the moral life, courtesy is morally obligatory. In communities that are united around a common understanding of what is important, manners and morals tend to form parts of a whole.

Loss of shared cultural values poses a threat to shared manners

Unlike the Orthodox, when we meet in a secular pluralist society, we have significant disagreements about how to be respectful or show courtesy, because we have significant disagreements about the nature of morality and the good life. Alasdair MacIntyre's description of our culture as no longer in possession of a common vision of virtue suggests as well a world without a common notion of manners[3] We meet in the ruins of previously intact social practices, among the shards of once well-functioning understandings of the human condition. Even the 'we' by which we describe ourselves has fragmented and become problematic. Though never have more people used European languages as their first or second idiom of expression, employed legal systems influenced by European-American jurisprudence, and been influenced by European-American economic and cultural styles (eg, from fast food to styles of dress), there is a reluctance to speak confidently from the perspective of European-American manners and morals. Indeed, confidence in European manners is for many a mark of an execrable cultural imperialism, rather than the celebration of cultural vigour and success. Though cultural differences have never been as muted as in our age of mass communication and mass marketing, though there has never been such a singularity of cultural perspective for world history and culture (eg, the United Nations and the International Court of Justice, which have some claim to being the assemblages of our planet, are the creations of Euro-American culture), there is ever more talk of moral diversity and cultural pluralism. Indeed, the systematic study of cultural differences along with their toleration is an innovation of European-American culture. Despite all of this, eurocentrism is a criticism rather than a ground of support for our manners.

Not only are our understandings of manners brought into question because of their special bond to the European roots of our cultures, not only does this bond invite the recognition of cultural differences, but in addition the notion of courtesy has an elitist valence. Manners are properly not the canons of common, vulgar behaviour. Courtesy is courtly politeness. Good manners express the rules of refined deportment, those of the court which sets the standard. Manners and courtesy are how the best people behave (or how they should behave) to each other. Manners are how those who have cultivated proper deportment show each other proper regard. Good manners acknowledge and aspire to an ideal of deportment, not the usual (ie, common or vulgar) patterns of behaviour. In their normative, not merely descriptive character, as well as because of their association with aristocracies and with those who rule, good manners are suspect.

For Western Europe the notion of courtesy has been ambiguous since the fall of the Empire in the West. *Homo romanus* understood what it was to act *humaniter*. *Humanitas* had been equivalent to *romanitas*. *Humanitas* incarnated what it was to have that refinement and grace of deportment, which contrasted with the behaviour of *homo barbarus*. All this began to pass with Alaric's sack of Rome. The arrogation of the imperial crown by Charles the Great on Christmas Day, AD 800, intimated the hope of a restoration. This was not to be. Step by step, with the weakening of the Western Empire following the Reformation, with the subsequent Pax Westfalica, and finally with the abdication of Emperor Francis II on 6th August, 1806, Europe separated ever more into diverse Europes and departing European colonies. The Reformation and the emergence of nation-states fractured the hope of a single European cultural perspective into several national cultures. Moreover, the nineteenth and twentieth centuries marked the canonization of class consciousness, class divisions, and class struggle, thus further dividing manners and bringing traditional canons of courtesy into question (eg, the salutation 'dear sir' was for some replaced by 'comrade').

Political Correctness sublimates traditional manners to a 'thin world culture'

Manners in their particularity separate. They announce commitments, including moral understandings, that collide with the commitments of others. One can only show consideration through particular forms and conventions. It is this particularity that vexes. For a gentleman to open a door for a lady or to kiss her hand can be regarded as sexist. For a Texan lady to walk to the right of the gentleman so that, should the occasion necessitate, he might more easily draw his revolver from his shoulder holster in defence can be regarded as an expression of false consciousness. To inquire whether one is dining according to the Spanish or the French court before opening a potato may be received as elitist. To date one's letters AD 1995, rather than 1995, can be appreciated as religiously insensitive ('1995 CE' can demonstrate a special delicacy). To say 'God bless' to a sneeze may evoke puzzlement. To require coat and tie at one's club can suggest a eurocentric sexism. And, *miserabile factu*, to fly the Stainless Banner on Confederate Memorial Day in remembrance of fallen heroes will likely be decried as racist.

While a certain thin world culture has emerged, still primarily framed in terms of European concerns, manners and morals have been politicized as our polities have broken into numerous and competing self-consciously diverse moral communities. In the face of this diversity, to act according to traditional manners can be received as a reactionary political manifesto. This is the character of post-modernity. A once officially homogeneous Christian culture has fragmented such that even reference to the West as Christendom is not merely appreciated as inaccurate but impolite, indeed, 'insensitive' and offensive. There is no longer a universal moral narrative, nor the secular resources for reclaiming a universal vision of proper deportment.[4]

We live in an age in which the received manners and morals of our culture are in disarray and under attack. We confront diverse and often mutually hostile visions of appropriate behaviour. Moreover, our traditional understandings of proper behaviour are frequently regarded as improper (ie, as being sexist, elitist, eurocentric, etc). In response to this challenge, canons of courtesy have been framed to share without the offence occasioned by particularity (eg, Christmas greetings become best wishes for a generic winter festival, Easter greetings become best wishes for a nameless spring festival, etc). It is with such vacuous understandings of courtesy that we communicate in the ruins of a once intact Western European morality and canon of manners.

Establishing manners between strangers
What are the good manners that can bind a feminist and a Southern gentleman, a proletarian and a titled lady? What common courtesy governs when individuals do not share a moral vision or a common understanding of the good life? How can individuals share manners when they confront each other across conflicting moral understandings and competing political visions? This daunting task of providing canons of appropriate politeness in such circumstances defines the project of civility in most secular pluralist societies. To establish such canons of courtesy, one must speak to the authority of their governance. But how does one do this, given our foundational controversies regarding the proper character of manners? How does one decide whose manners are normative — those of the feminist or the Southern gentleman, the proletarian or the titled lady?

As with moral controversies, controversies regarding good manners can be solved by appeals: to force; to faith; to rational argument; or to agreement (including agreement peaceably not to agree).[5] Force may be an effective short-term means of suppressing controversies in manners. One can impose a particular understanding of courtesy. But this will not by itself provide either intellectual or moral satisfaction. This is not to say that one cannot show good manners in war or in a combat to the death. Individuals entering into a duel can find themselves united in common understandings of appropriate manners, even if they have resolved to conclude a controversy through force. Indeed, going to the field of honour to resolve a controversy presupposes a common sense of honour and with it common standards of appropriate deportment. Such standards guide those involved, even when they acknowledge that these activities are immoral. In order with others to distinguish honourable from dishonourable uses of force, one must already share a common vision of courtesy.

Rationality not sufficient for manners between strangers
The appeal to a particular vision of proper conduct presupposes faith in this vision. Such a commitment can arise from being born into as well as later converting to a particular vision of appropriate behaviour. As with matters of religion and morals, if one deports oneself well according to a particular set of manners, others may adopt those practices. They may appreciate an excellence to which they ought to

aspire. Though such conversions may resolve some controversies regarding appropriate manners by bringing some individuals into concord, the general incivility of the world, as well as the class of contrary visions of appropriate canons of courtesy, suggests that an appeal to conversion will not generally be sufficient for the difficulties at hand.

An attempt to resolve controversies regarding proper canons of courtesy through rational argument will not succeed unless one already shares a common background understanding of values. One cannot compare the consequences of particular canons of deportment unless one already understands how to assess such consequences. How does one, for example, compare the consequences of frankness in speech with the solidarity and support conveyed by the polite euphemisms that protect against hurt feelings? Such comparisons can only proceed if one already understands how to rank or compare different interests and goals. Yet those in dispute often fail to share common visions of what is at stake, much less how to resolve the controversies at hand. If one shares sufficient background premises, rules of evidence, rules of inference, then sound rational argument can give guidance regarding the canons of courtesy one should embrace. But the more this is lacking, the more one will meet as strangers disunited in manners and behaviour.

Problem of regaining manners in a post-modern society without shared values

Those who meet in the conflicts of post-modernity are often separated by incommensurable visions of proper human conduct and human flourishing. They meet as strangers, as persons whose morals and manners are alien to each other. To be strangers, they need not be so alien as to be incomprehensible to each other. It is enough if the others, who appear as strangers, assemble the important elements of the good life and proper manners in substantially wrong ways. One can understand them and in understanding disagree and perceive a deep gulf of manners and sensibilities. Yet one does not share enough in common to resolve controversies by sound rational argument. In intact moral communities with functioning traditions, one can have the friendship of common understandings of courtesy. Outside of one's community of shared manners and morals, one meets those who find one's courtesies alien, strange, if not profoundly misguided. The 'other' appears not only strange but often hostile: a person denying one's manners as well as the values and social structures for which they stand.

Common cause, and shared manners, require appeal to the authority of the participants

How does one resolve controversies regarding courtesy with those strange to one's commitments? If one does not share a common vision of courtesy, and if one wishes to resolve controversies with an authority other than force, then one can appeal to the authority of common agreement. Insofar as one acts together in agreement, one possesses authority drawn from mutual consent. Insofar as individuals peaceably withdraw to their own communities, the very practice of resolving controversies by common agreement, not force, restrains one from interfering. Authority grounded in the sparseness of consent frames contracts, the market, and the foundations of limited democracies. The authority of such practices is derived from an appeal neither to God nor to rational argument, but to the agreement of those who participate. In such circumstances, common projects can be undertaken with authority, but they will in principle be limited by the limited character of the agreements of those who entered into such undertakings. Forbearance rights and limited welfare rights will be recognized, but they will not be grounded in a thick vision of human flourishing. Rather, their legitimacy will be derived from what it means to acknowledge persons as the source of authoritative consent.[6] Courtesy will not derive its authority from tradition or from a content-full moral view, but from the tacit consent to various practices that develop in social interaction.

Manners for cosmopolitans: shared values replaced by bureaucracy

Against this thin morality, which is background to the market and limited democracies, what can one say of manners? What role can courtesy play? When one meets as moral strangers in the marketplace, as well as in the public assemblies of limited democracies, there will often be advantages in preserving peace and supporting the limited exchange of views required for the functioning of limited projects. Rules of procedure, rules of order, bureaucratic safeguards, and the courtesies associated with due process will tend to frame the canons of civil deportment for such circumstances. A bureaucratic courtesy emerges in which dates appear as 1995, as neither AD 1995 nor 1995

CE. There is a language of studied politeness neither aristocratic nor proletarian (toilets are for men or women, not for ladies or gentlemen). Women are Ms, never Mrs or Miss unless they insist on what some would insist is an anachronism. There is a polished attention to avoid a clash of cultures and moralities occasioned by a clash of contrary courtesies.

Canons of effective advertising will often underlie the canons of common courtesy.[7] After all, expressions of gratitude, solicitude, and interest can function to reinforce market transactions. Many may trade more willingly if they not only are treated honestly, but are also offered products and services within frameworks of civility and respect. Given our divergent notions of civility and respect, expressions of courtesy must be as vacuous and general in character as possible. One avoids wishing a Merry Christmas or Happy Easter but announces instead one's best wishes for the holidays. Any offence may impose market costs. The result is a practised general politeness without particular tradition or history. In such a world there are no Christian gentlemen, only good gentlepersons.

Bankruptcy of cosmopolitan manners when divorced from tradition

A courtesy that aspires to be polite to everyone is polished courtesy without substance.[8] Indeed, because of its commitment to generality, cosmopolitan manners runs the risk of encouraging a hostility to those courtesies designed to communicate tradition and substance. The courtesy that attempts to be polite to everyone is ideally a courtesy of nowhere and no time. It is in its very nature hostile to traditions. This genre of manners is embedded in what Alasdair MacIntyre characterizes as a cosmopolitan culture articulated in an international language of modernity. In a post-modern world sharing no substantive moral narrative or vision, the remaining aspiration of modernity is to a civility that can bind moral strangers and be expressed in a language without particular commitments.

> The social and cultural condition of those who speak that kind of language [is] a certain type of rootless cosmopolitanism, the condition of those who aspiring to be at home anywhere — except that is, of course, in what they regard as the backward, outmoded, undeveloped cultures of traditions — are therefore in an important way citizens of nowhere...It is the fate toward which modernity

> moves precisely insofar as it successfully modernizes itself and others by emancipating itself from social, cultural, and linguistic particularity and so from tradition.[9]

The manners of cosmopolitans are sufficiently vacuous as to betoken only the most general respect for the other. It is a courtesy that expresses respect without giving any content to respect.

Substantive understandings of courtesy break the generality of cosmopolitan aspirations. It is for this reason that, from the perspective of cosmopolitans, substantive practices and traditions of courtesy run the risk of being insensitive, indeed, politically incorrect. Substantive understandings of manners can only bind those with whom one shares traditions, customs, and, ideally, content-full moral principles. Such manners are the forms of courtesy that reveal the other either as a stranger to one's traditions, or as a friend to one's commitments in manners, if not in morals. Such substantive understandings run the risk of appearing not just insensitive but fanatical, because they recall individuals to particular communities and traditions. From the perspective of the cosmopolitan, the politeness that binds moral friends within substantive moral traditions will often be experienced as an enemy of peace in a world too often rent by moral particularity and the misunderstandings and conflicts they can engender.

Manners toward strangers: traditionally seen as a moral imperative

From the perspective of moral friends, especially those who share traditional moral understandings and manners, the manners that bind moral strangers are unavoidable. They are also occasions of moral compromise. Even if one lives one's life among the Amish or Hassidim, one must enter the market with those hostile to one's moral commitments and communicate through manners which avoid reference to the matters one takes to be most important. This is morally tolerable, as long as one distinguishes between the manners one shares with strangers and those one shares with friends. Most importantly, one must not confuse the manners of moral strangers with the manners of moral friends. One must not mistakenly conclude that the courtesy that guides in the marketplace or in the *agora* of secular pluralist democracies should be the manners that should bind in the important friendships that unite around substantive traditions. The cost of such a mistake is the loss of substance and tradition in the manners of one's life.

In the ruins, within the market, behind the walls

In many respects, our situation is like that of our forebears a millennium and a half ago, as the Empire in the West fell into chaos. Those who could retreated to their villas, which became fortifications in Britain and in Gaul against a tide of chaos and pillage. If all could not be saved, at least remnants of civilization could be preserved. Even if civility was temporarily in retreat, there was still the hope that it could be sustained behind the walls of particular communities bent on preserving what was important.

One might think of the description given by Sidonius Apollinarius (430-483) during this period of transition. The account is probably from between AD 462 and 467. It tells of a visit to a villa that was maintaining its treasures and the traditional civilities despite the collapse of the Empire.

> I have spent the most delicious time in visiting two charming properties and two most sympathetic hosts... Hardly had I entered one vestibule or the other when behold!...[in one] part were books in any number ready to hand; you might have imagined yourself looking at the shelves of a professional scholar or at the tiers in the Athenaeum or at the towering presses of the booksellers... — here Augustine, there Varro, here Horace, there Prudentius...We would all join in a discussion expressing our various views just as we felt inclined...[T]he head cook had his eye on the passage of the hours as marked by the water-clock, and as the fifth hour was just departing he was proved to have arrived just at the right moment. The luncheon was at once short and lavish, in the style of senators, who have an inherited and established practice of having abundant viands served up on a few dishes, although the meal is varied by having some of the meats roasted and others stewed...To sum up, our entertainment was moral, elegant, and profuse.[10]

Against great difficulties, a remnant of *humanitas* and *romanitas* had been preserved. Romulus Augustulus was yet to abdicate in 476. There was nearly a millennium before that dreadful Tuesday of May 29, 1453.

Manners ultimately only possible with the preservation of a civilized moral society

In many ways we who have content-full understandings of civility, courtesy, and manners are like the owners of that villa. If we are to preserve them, we must find a place where they can be protected, nurtured and sustained. Our life of manners is bifurcated. We must distinguish the context in which they can still thrive from the context in which they are given no place. If we confuse the two contexts, we will endanger the civility and manners of our surviving traditions. Those who enter the market or the general transactions of a limited democracy participate in a vacuous fabric of courtesies aimed at showing respect, gratitude and solidarity without promoting contention. On the other hand, those who belong to content-full traditions have rich notions of proper deportment, which to some will be offensive. Such thick understandings of courtesy will be affirmed within the bounds of particular communities. Manners are no longer whole and of one piece. There are the manners through which one collaborates with strangers. There are manners that bind friends in common understandings of the good life. Courtesy has become contextual and freighted with controversy.

Notes and References

Chapter 1

1. Nathanial Hawthorne, 'Feathertop: A Moralized Legend', in *Mosses from an Old Manse*, 1846; in Centenary Edition, Ohio State University Press, 1974, vol X.
2. E P Thompson, *The Poverty of Theory*, Merlin Press, 1978, p 153.
3. Charles Kingsley, *Yeast*, John W Parker, 1851, pp 295-6.
4. Shirley Robin Letwin, *The Gentleman in Trollope: Individuality and Moral Conduct*, Macmillan, 1992, p 10.
5. Quoted in Letwin, ibid, p 6.
6. F Wills, *'What is a Gentleman?' Lay Sermons*, Griffith, Farran Okeden & Welsh, 1890, p 42.
7. G P Marsh, *Lectures in the English Language*, John Murray, 1862, p 437.
8. *The Spectator*, February 2, 1901, p 170.
9. Quoted in Letwin, op cit, p 6.
10. Richard Steele, *The Spectator*, 1711, no 75.
11. Charles Strachey (ed), *The letters of the Earl of Chesterfield to his son*, Methuen, 1901, letter cxlvi, vol I, p 284.
12. Thomas Gainsford, *The Rich Cabinet*, Roger Jackson, 1616, p 56 verso.
13. W R Browne, 'The English Gentleman', in *National Review*, April 1886, pp 263-4.
14. W M Thackeray, *Works*, Smith, Elder & Co, 1883, vol ix, p 517.
15. K Smith, *The Spectator*, January 12, 1907.
16. Browne, op cit, p 264.
17. Andrew St George, *The Descent of Manners*, Chatto & Windus, 1993, p xi.
18. 'Mind your Manners', in *Household Words*, 1885, vol x, p 386.
19. J R Vernon, *Contemporary Review*, 1869, xi, p 572.
20. Strachey, op cit, letter cc, vol I, p 386.
21. J Swift, 'On Good Manners and Good Breeding', *Works*, (edited by Herbert Davis, Blackwell, 1957), vol IV, pp 213-4.
22. J Boswell, *Journal of a Tour of the Hebrides*, August 2, 1773.
23. Strachey, op cit, letter cclxxvii, vol II, p 228.
24. William Empson, *Milton's God*, Chatto & Windus, 1965, p 28.

25. Mrs Craik, *John Halifax, Gentleman*, Pocket Classics, Alan Sutton, 1991, ch XVII, p 209.
26. Mrs Jenner, *An Imperfect Gentleman*, Longmans, Green & Co, 1888, iii, p 306.
27. J H Friswell, *The Gentle Life*, Samson, Low, Son, & Marston, 1864, p 31.
28. Mary Linskell, *In Exchange for a Soul*, Chatto & Windus, 1887, vol I, pp 197-8.

Chapter 5

1. A Coffin Hanson, *Manet and the Modern Tradition*, Yale University Press, 1979, p 19.
2. J Laver, *Taste and Fashion from the French Revolution to the Present Day*, George G Harrap and Co, 1945 (first published 1937).
3. For a defence of modern manners of dress as a necessary part of modern democracy, see G Lipovetsky, *The Empire of Fashion: Dressing Modern Democracy* (trans: C Porter), Princeton, 1994.
4. R Scruton, *The Aesthetics of Architecture*, Methuen, 1979, p 33.
5. B Martin, *A Sociology of Contemporary Cultural Change*, Basil Blackwell, 1983.
6. W Pater, *Marius the Epicurean*, Penguin, 1985 p 112.
7. C D'Souza, 'Face facts', *Sunday Times Style*, December 18, 1994.
8. R A D Grant, *Conservative Thoughts: Essays from the Salisbury Review*, The Claridge Press, 1988, p 17.

Chapter 6

1. BBC, 'Breakfast News', October 11, 1994.
2. *Sunday Times*, February 26, 1984.
3. A change analysed in Graeme Wright, *Betrayal: The Struggle for Cricket's Soul*, London: H F & G Witherby, 1993, esp cchs 1, 2 and 3; on Hughes see Simon Wilde, *Letting Rip: The Fast Bowling Threat from Lillee to Waqar*, London: H F & G Witherby, 1994, pp 124-6; on Warner, see *inter alia* Ronald Mason, *Plum Warner's Last Season (1920)*, London: 1970, Epworth Press, esp ch 2; and on Trumper, the various essays in Vasant Raiji (ed), *Victor Trumper: The Beau Ideal of a Cricketer*, Bombay: Oxford University Press, 1964, esp chs 9 and 10.
4. Trevor Bailey, 'Peter May: The Amateur with the Professional Approach', in idem, *The Greatest of My Time*, London: Eyre and Spottiswoode, 1968, pp 74-81, at p 80.
5. *The Daily Telegraph*, December 28, 1994. See also the appreciation by E W Swanton, in the same newspaper on the same day.
6. Bailey, op cit, pp 80-1.
7. Cited in Jack Fingleton, *Batting from Memory*, London: Hodder and Stoughton, 1981, p 119.
8. Donald Bradman, *A Farewell to Cricket*, London: Hodder and Stoughton, 1950, p 214.

9. Douglas Sutherland, *The English Gentleman*, London: Debrett, 1978, p xi.
10. Letwin, op cit, p 3; my debt to this work more generally will be obvious in what immediately follows.
11. A phrase attributed to Archbishop William Temple (1881-1944); the source is unknown.
12. Letwin, op cit, pp 4-6; citing G Sitwell, 'The English Gentleman', *The Ancestor*, no 1, 1902, pp 58-103 and A Wagner, *Heralds and Heraldry in the Middle Ages*, Oxford: Oxford University Press, 1939, *English Genealogy*, Oxford: Oxford University Press, 1960 and *English Ancestry*, Oxford: Oxford University Press, 1961.
13. Alexis de Tocqueville, *On the State of Society in France before the Revolution of 1789* (trans: Henry Reeve) London: John Murray, 1856, pp 151-6 and 179-81.
14. Auguste de Staël-Holstein, *Letters on England*, 2nd ed, with additional letters and a life of the author by the Duchess of Broglie, London: Treuttel and Wurz, 1830, pp 132-3.
15. Letwin, op cit, pp 9-10; citing de Staël-Holstein, ibid, pp 124-5, 130, 131-2, 136 and 137.
16. As exemplified by the appalling Melmotte in Anthony Trollope's *The Way We Live Now*, 1875.
17. On the concept of 'civility' more generally, see the various essays collected in Edward C Banfield (ed), *Civility and Citizenship in Liberal Democratic Societies*, New York: Paragon House, 1992.
18. Letwin, op cit, pp 11-12.
19. Anon, 'The Historic Peerage of England', *Quarterly Review*, vol 103, 1858, pp 28-65, at p 39.
20. Letwin, op cit, p 18.
21. S T Coleridge, 'Letter to a Lady', *Biographia Literaria*; or *Biographical sketches of my literary life and opinions*, London: Rest Fenner, 1817, vol 2, pp 208-9.
22. Letwin, op cit, p 19.
23. Hippolyte Taine, *Notes on England* (trans: E Hyams) London: Thames and Hudson, 1957, p 144.
24. For a modern, general account of this phenomenon, see Keith Robbins, *Nineteenth-Century Britain: England, Scotland and Wales; The Making of a Nation*, Oxford: Oxford University Press, 1989, ch 6.
25. Delabere P Blaine, 'Cricket', in idem, *An Encyclopaedia of Rural Sports; Or, A Complete Account, Historical, Practical and Descriptive of Hunting, Shooting, Fishing, Racing, etc, etc*, 2nd ed, London: Longman, Brown, Green, and Longmans 1852, pp 134-6 and p 139.
26. Anon, 'Cricket: The Premier Game of England', in Various, *Encyclopedia of Sport, Games and Pastimes*, London: Fleetway House, 1935, p 187; the best 'history' for this period remains H S Altham, *A History of Cricket: From the Beginnings to the First World War*, London: George Allen and Unwin, 1962, esp pts 1 and 2.
27. Edward Lyttelton, *Memories and Hopes*, London: John Murray, 1925, p 6.

28. David Lemmon, *Percy Chapman,* London: Queen Anne Press, 1985, p 10.
29. *Daily Telegraph*, October 16, 1895; private information.
30. Blain, op cit, pp 134-6; see also the remarks in W J Ford, 'Cricket', in the Earl of Suffolk and Berkshire (ed), *The Encylcopaedia of Sports and Games*, Vol 1, 2nd ed, London: Heinemann, 1911, pp 439-40.
31. Neville Cardus, *English Cricket*, London: Collins, 1945, p 7.
32. The word was used by Stanley Baldwin, "Cricket", in idem, *Our Inheritance*, London: Hodder and Stoughton, pp 298-300, at p 300.
33. James D Coldham, *Lord Harris*, London: George Allen and Unwin, 1989, pp 5-6.
34. Evelyn Waugh, *A Little Learning*, London: Chapman and Hall, 1964, p 68.
35. For a recent account of tennis and gentility, see E Digby Baltzell, *Sporting Gentlemen: Men's tennis from the age of honour to the cult of the superstar*, New York: Free Press, 1995, esp chs 3 and 4.
36. Ford, op cit, p 459.
37. Charles Cowden Clarke, 'Introduction', to John Nyren, *The Young Cricketer's Tutor*, 2nd ed, London: Effingham Wilson, 1893, p 7.
38. A S Ranjitsinhji, 'Batting' in Suffolk and Berkshire, op cit, p 460.
39. Blaine, op cit, p 136.
40. T Richardson, 'Fast Bowling', in Suffolk and Berkshire, op cit, p 469.
41. Ford, op cit, p 449.
42. Richardson, op cit, p 469.
43. David Frith, *The Fast Men: A Two Hundred Year Cavalcade of Speed Bowlers*, London: Queen Anne Press, 1975, p 70.
44. The finest life remains Ronald Mason, *Jack Hobbs*, London: Hollis and Carter, 1960, passim.
45. Jean Fayard, quoted in Allen Synge (ed), *Stranger's Gallery: some foreign views of English cricket*, London: Lemon Tree Press, 1974, pp 116-117.
46. Quoted in Richard Buckle, *Nijinsky*, London: Weidenfeld and Nicolson, 1971, p 287.
47. F G J Ford, 'County Cricket', in Suffolk and Berkshire, op cit, p 481.
48. Bobbie Burlton, *Cricketing Courtesy: Manners, Customs, Etiquette*, Bromsgrove: privately printed, 1954, p 3.
49. Ibid, pp 20-1.
50. Ibid, pp 23-5.
51. Ibid, p 17.
52. Ibid, p 10.
53. Ibid, p 27.
54. Ibid, p 25.
55. Ibid.
56. Quoted in Keith Dunstan, *Sports*, Melbourne: Odhams, 1973, p 115.
57. Peter Baxter, 'Turning the Clock Back', *Sunday Telegraph*, January 22, 1995, provides a recent account of those events, to which I am much indebted; for Jardine's own view, see D R Jardine, *In Quest of the Ashes*, London:

Hutchinson & Co, 1933, esp 'Dedication' and ch xi; and, for an Australian opinion, J H W Fingleton, *Cricket Crisis*, London: Cassell, 1947, *passim.*

58. Charles Richmond Thatcher, 'Cricket', nd; cited in Stephen Murray-Smith, *The Dictionary of Australian Quotations*, London: Heinemann, 1984, p 261.
59. On which, see A J Forrest, *Village Cricket*, London: Robert Hale, 1957, passim.
60. G M Trevelyan, *English Social History*, London: Longman, Green & Co, 1944, p 408.
61. Coldham, op cit, p 86-7.
62. Anon, *Encyclopedia of Sports, Games and Pastimes*, op cit, p 187.
63. Cited in Robert Andrews (ed), *The Routledge Dictionary of Quotations*, London: Routledge Kegan Paul, 1987, p 57.
64. On Hawke, see James P Coldham, *Lord Hawke: A Cricketing Biography*, London: Crowood Press, 1990, esp ch 14.
65. C P Snow, *The Search*, London: Victor Gollancz, 1934, pp 242-4.
66. Martin Green, *Children of the Sun: a narrative of 'decadence' in England after 1918*, London: Constable, 1977, pp 59-60.

Chapter 8

1. Surprisingly, Mill had earlier argued in his 1840 essay on Coleridge that, in any society held together by allegiance, there must be '*something* which is settled, something permanent, and not to be called into question: something which, by general agreement, has a right to be where it is, and to be secure against disturbance'.
2. See John Gray, 'Toleration', in Digby Anderson (ed), *The Loss of Virtue*, SAU and *National Review*, London, 1993.
3. The writer, says Johnson again, 'solicits fame at the hazard of disgrace'. Those who seek esteem beyond the minimum due to ordinary unassuming members of society cannot complain if society declines to confer it, or worse, punishes their presumption by withholding even that minimum.
4. Historical 'truth', Oakeshott observes, is no more than 'what the evidence obliges us to believe'. Note, however, that whatever it is, we are still *obliged* to believe it.
5. The ethical and human problems created by these rigorous professional conventions have never to my knowledge been better illustrated than by Dickens in *Great Expectations*, in the character of the star defence lawyer Jaggers. Rightly calculating that most of his clients will be guilty, he refuses to let them admit anything compromising, even to him, so that his integrity in contending for their innocence shall not itself be compromised.
6. One of Alciati's *Emblems* (1531) says that the learned should not speak ill of each other (*doctos doctis obloqui nefas*), though perhaps this was merely to protect their mystery against a hostile world.
7. This is not because most academics on appointments or promotion committees are themselves radicals, but because they are afraid of being accused of illiberalism, or of siding with it, by the few who are. The latter

thus exercise an unofficial power of veto.

8. In his lively and engaging book *The Unnatural Nature of Science*, Lewis Wolpert has recently pointed out that genuine scientific thinking is virtually the opposite of common sense. This is absolutely not the case with the humanities. There common sense, though it may not be everything, is as indispensable as in everyday life.
9. A E Housman observed of the notorious eighteenth-century classicist Richard Bentley that no man was ever better equipped to discover the truth and none more indifferent to doing so.
10. Cf note 1 above.
11. The world of the humanities is the world of human desire and human interest generally, but that does not mean it cannot be approached in a spirit of objectivity. What matters is that our own purely personal preferences should colour our perceptions as little as possible, and that we should be careful not to treat them as values, even if they are. The personal preference of the virtuous will be for objective values, certainly; but the point is precisely to exclude personal preference. Hitler was without question a bad man, and National Socialism an evil system; but those undoubted facts add nothing to our historical understanding of Nazi Germany, and, if we allow them to do so, may do much to muddy it.
12. I have touched on this point in 'Freedom For What?' in G Anderson and M Kaplan (eds), *Morality and Religion in Liberal Democratic Societies*, New York: Paragon House, 1991.
13. For some inconclusive observations concerning these tendencies, see my review of Michael Oakeshott's posthumous *Religion, Politics and the Moral Life*, in the *Times Literary Supplement*, 15th April, 1994. They may well be mere sentimental religiosity, conveniently disencumbered of any clear, unequivocal moral imperatives. On the other hand, they may equally amount to a revival of concrete, practical and pre-doctrinal *pietas*.
14. On what counts as 'truth' and in what senses it does, see Cardinal Newman, *A Grammar of Assent*. On truth as subjective conviction, see Kierkegaard generally.
15. Shaw's *St Joan* is intolerably sentimental (particularly at the end), but it also gives us an arresting view of the genuine disinterestedness, patience and indeed altruism of Joan's inquisitors, who are desperate to save her from damnation as a heretic.
16. Before he secured the intellectual credit he has now once again forfeited, Freud was wont to accuse his critics of 'unconscious resistance'. This of course is a perfect text-book example of unfalsifiability.
17. Perhaps the most important of these passions is sentimentality. Before the advent of penicillin an even more horrible affliction, syphilis, had claimed and was claiming infinitely more lives than AIDS. But no one wore a 'syphilis ribbon' or unfurled a 'syphilis quilt' on the Mall in Washington, even though the disease had been acquired in a similar, if sexually less unorthodox, manner. Nor would they now do so, if syphilis were still rife. Nor would

anyone be wearing AIDS ribbons and the rest if AIDS cases, though no less numerous than now, were confined merely to drug users and recipients of infected blood. Why?

18. Many years ago a young colleague, who till then had woodenly subscribed to every right-on permutation of Marxism, feminism and post-structuralism on offer, and had (to my mind) displayed not the slightest intelligence on any topic whatever, was suddenly visited, over mid-morning coffee, by a remarkable revelation. 'Mind you, if Derrida's right,' she announced slowly, peering through her John Lennon glasses darkly and dragging meaningfully on her scrawny liquorice-paper roll-up, 'it means we can't protest about the Bomb.' This must have been a good two years before the now Warton Professor of English at Oxford, Terry Eagleton, informed us that although deconstruction was fine for exploding bourgeois ideology, we ought to keep it well away from Marxism, which of course really is true.
19. K Minogue, *The Concept of a University*, Weidenfeld and Nicolson, 1973, p 157. I have not re-read this excellent book since it came out, but I am sure that I owe it a great deal more than this little phrase about Marx, which I have just tracked down.
20. His central contention, on which the entire Marxian thesis depends, is the labour theory of value. But this had been pretty conclusively refuted by a run-of-the-mill economist of the 1830s, Archbishop Whately, who observed that pearls were not expensive because men dived for them, but rather that men were prepared to dive for them because they were expensive.
21. As I recall, this was one of Minogue's central points. (See note 19 above.)

Chapter 10

1. D Martin, *Tracts Against the Times*, London: Lutterworth, 1973, p 29.
2. Even the Chief Executive of Barclay's Bank tells us that 'British capitalism's rejection of social values and reaction against earlier [socialist] collective excesses has gone too far. Too much individualism is bad for too many individuals', *Financial Times*, March 16, 1995, p 14.
3. In addition to the nineteenth-century thinkers mentioned in the next sentence, the following mid-twentieth-century thinkers deserve notice and credit for having foreseen and warned about anarchic tendencies and developments that are now bearing terrible fruit: T S Eliot, *Christianity and Culture*, New York: Harcourt Brace, 1939, 1948; E von Kuehnelt-Leddihn, *Liberty or Equality*, 1952, new ed, Front Vale, VA: Christendom, 1993; Robert Nisbet, *The Quest for Community*, 1953, new ed, San Francisco: ICS Press, 1990; Russell Kirk, *The Conservative Mind*, 1953, 7th rev ed, Washington DC: Regnery Gateway, 1986.
4. Robert Pattison, *The Great Dissent: John Henry Newman and the Liberal Heresy*, New York: Oxford University Press, 1991, p 179. For a mordant comment on Rorty's 'anti-foundationalism' see p 213. For a thoroughgoing critique of the 'rationalistic antinomianism' of J S Mill and his school of liberalism, see Maurice Cowling, *Mill and Liberalism*, 1963, 2nd ed,

Cambridge University Press, 1990.

5. 'Everything that liberates our minds without at the same time adding to our resources of self-mastery is evil'. Goethe quoted in Erich Heller, *Atlantic Brief Lives*, Boston: Little, Brown and Co, 1965, pp 324-5.
6. Quoted in Pattison, op cit, pp 178-9. 'The modern fanatic is a radical skeptic', Philip Rieff, *Fellow Teachers*, Chicago: University of Chicago Press, 1985, p XIII.
7. See, eg, 'Honor Thy Children', *US News and World Report*, February 27, 1995, pp 39 ff; William Raspberry, 'Victims of a Failed Revolution', *International Herald Tribune*, April 5, 1995, p 9; Raspberry 'Dad is gone, and so is social cohesion', *Daily Progress*, Charlottesville VA, March 14, 1993; Philip Jenkins's review of Lawrence Stone's *The Road to Divorce: England 1530-1987* (Oxford 1990), in *The Chesterton Review*, 18,1, February 1992, pp 104-7; David Blankenhorn, *Fatherless America: Confronting Our Most Urgent Social Problem*, New York: Harper Collins/Basic Books, 1995; Susan Chira, 'America's Growing Ranks: Children of Divorce', *International Herald Tribune*, March 27, 1995, p 16.
8. Halsey, quoted by Lynette Burrows, London *Sunday Telegraph*, July 21, 1991, p 20. On illegitimacy rates, see *The American Enterprise*, Washington DC, 6,1, Jan-Feb, 1995, p 41.
9. Rosalind Miles, *The Children We Deserve*, London: Harper Collins, 1994, quoted by Minette Martin, London *Sunday Telegraph*, July 17, 1994, p 9.
10. Bell, *The Cultural Contradictions of Capitalism*, New York: Basic Books, 1978; Lasch, *The Culture of Narcissism*, New York: Warner, 1979; Postman, *Technopoly*, New York: Random House, 1992.
11. Aldous Huxley's *Brave New World* (1932) was prophetic in this respect. In addition to Postman's book (n 10), the earlier work of Jacques Ellul, *The Technological Society*, New York: Knopf, 1954, retains a fundamental importance that was recognized by Huxley, who was instrumental in getting it translated and published in English. See also, M D Aeschliman, *The Restitution of Man: C S Lewis and the Case Against Scientism*, Grand Rapids, Michigan: Eerdmans, 1983.
12. The sociologist James D Hunter has done the most to popularize and formulate the 'culture wars' motif. See *Culture Wars: The Struggle to Define America*, New York: Harper Collins/Basic Books, 1991. On 'legitimacy crises' see, *inter alia*, Peter Berger et al, *The Homeless Mind: Modernization and Consciousness*, New York: Random House, 1973; Richard J Neuhaus, *The Naked Public Square*, 2nd ed, Grand Rapids: Eerdmans, 1986; and James D Hunter and Stephen C Ainlay (eds), *Making Sense of Modern Times*, London: Routledge and Kegan Paul, 1986, pp 20-23 *et passim*.
13. Nisbet, *The Twilight of Authority*, New York: Oxford University Press, 1975. On the social importance of the family, see esp pp 252-260. The family 'remains the greatest single element of a creative culture' (p 255). Another fine, neglected book on authority — both warning and prophecy — is Thomas Molnar, *Authority and Its Enemies*, New Rochelle, NY: Arlington

House, 1976. See also Philip Rieff, eg, *Fellow Teachers*, op cit, esp pp X-XI, 67. For a first-rate critique of the pathologies of 'progressive' intellectuals, see Paul Johnson, *Intellectuals*, London: Weidenfeld and Nicolson, 1988.

14. L Stein (1958), quoted by Dennis Wrong in *Power: Its Forms, Bases and Uses*, Oxford: Blackwell, 1979, p 35.
15. Cf S S Acquaviva, *The Decline of the Sacred in Industrial Society*, ET, Oxford: Blackwell, 1979, pp 136-7. Monogamy and the family also domesticate, socialize and civilize *men*. See George Gilder, *Men and Marriage*, Gretna, Louisiana: Pelican, 1986.
16. On the value and importance — and inevitability, for good and for ill — of 'prejudices', see Wilfred Ward, 'The Functions of Prejudice', *Dublin Review*, vol 138, January 1906, pp 99-108; and Christopher Ricks, *T S Eliot and Prejudice*, London: Faber and Faber, 1988; and cf Newman: 'If we insist on proofs for everything, we shall never come to action: to act you must assume, and that assumption is faith'. 'The Tamworth Reading Room' in *Discussions and Arguments on Various Subjects*, London: Longmans, Green, 1885, p 295 (1st published 1841).
17. Trilling, 'Wordsworth and the Iron Time', 1951, reprinted in M H Abrams (ed), *Wordsworth: A Collection of Critical Essays*, Englewood Cliffs, NJ: Prentice-Hall, 1972, p 63.
18. For a short, superbly judicious discussion of social and political as well as literary issues raised here, see Eugene Genovese, *The Southern Tradition: The Achievement and Limitations of An American Conservatism*, Cambridge, Mass: Harvard University Press, 1994.
19. Anderson, 'Whitman's New Man', Introduction to Walt Whitman, *Walt Whitman;s Revision of the Analysis of 'Leaves of Grass'*, New York: New York University Press, 1974, p 19. Also see Anderson's *The Imperial Self*, New York: Knopf, 1971; and Lasch, op cit, esp pp 35-6.
20. Quoted by André Maurois, *Disraeli: A Picture of the Victorian Age*, 1927, tr Hamish Miles, New York: Time Life Books, 1965, p 292. On the passage to modern aestheticism, see Bell, op cit; Gertrude Himmelfarb, 'From Clapham to Bloomsbury: A Genealogy of Morals', in *Marriage and Morals Among the Victorians*, New York: Knopf, 1986; and Rieff, *Fellow Teachers*, op cit.
21. *Brave New World*, (1932), New York: Harper and Row Perennial Library, 1969, ch 3, pp 26-7.
22. Paraphrased in John Lukacs, *The Passing of the Modern Age*, New York: Harper and Row, 1970, p 82.
23. *The American Enterprise*, Washington DC, 6, 1 Jan-Feb 1995, p 37. See also Genovese's recent *The Southern Tradition*, op cit; and cf Monica Furlong: 'The best arguments in favor of marriage and family life are not that they promote happiness and reduce loneliness, though at their best they do these things, but that they create a situation in which facing the truth about ourselves — our self-deceiving, touchy, vain, inflated selves — becomes more difficult to avoid than it is anywhere else'. *Contemplating Now*, Philadelphia: Westminster, 1971, p 118.

24. There is a great and valuable literature here, which someday may be recovered. Its starting point is *I'll Take My Stand: The South and the Agrarian Tradition*, 1930, by 'Twelve Southerners' (who included some of the most distinguished American writers of the twentieth century); see the recent edition with an introduction by Louis D Rubin, Jr, Baton Rouge: Louisiana State University Press, 1977. See also *Why the South Will Survive: Fifteen Southerners Look at Their Region a Half Century after "I'll Take My Stand"*, Athens, Georgia: University of Georgia Press, 1981; and, *inter alia*, Eugene Genovese, op cit; G M Curtis and J J Thompson (eds), *The Southern Essays of Richard M Weaver*, Indianapolis: Liberty Press, 1987; M E Bradford, *Generations of the Faithful Heart: On the Literature of the South*, La Salle, Illinois: Sherwood Sugden, 1983; and, more generally, Louis D Rubin et al (eds), *The History of Southern Literature*, Baton Rouge, Louisiana: Louisiana State University Press, 1985, in which the following apt assertion is made by Cleanth Brooks: 'A true community (*Gemeinschaft*) is held together by manners and morals deriving from a commonly held view of reality' -a *res publica* (p 339).
25. Allen Tate, *The Fathers*, (1938) Chicago: Swallow 1984. See also Radcliffe Squires, *Allen Tate: A Literary Biography*, New York: Pegasus, 1971.
26. Cf Tate, *The Fathers*, op cit: 'it is said by other authors than Apollonius that Jason desecrated his fathers' graves. I have no doubt that he did.' (p 268). For the significance of the 1960s, see Norman Podharet, 'A Monument to Jack Kerouac?' *Washington Post*, January 8, 1987; Christopher Booker, *The Neophiliacs*, 1969; Bston: Gambit, 1970; Morris Dickstein, *Gates of Eden: American Culture in the Sixties*, 1977; New York: Penguin, 1979; and Peter Collier and David Horowitz, *Destructive Generation: Second Thoughts about the '60s*, New York: Simon and Schuster/Summit, 1989. Cf also Laschi, op cit — and Turgenev's *Fathers and Sons*, 1861. Daniel Bell (op cit, p168) writes: 'What is being sought today in the phrase of Alexander Mitscherlich, is a "society without fathers".'
27. F Dostoevsky, *The Diary of a Writer*, quoted in *The American Scholar*, 64,1, Winter 1995, p 142.
28. Ibid.
29. Ibid.
30. Acquaviva, op cit, p 136.
31. Dostoevsky, op cit, p 142. Cf the Black essayist William Raspberry, 'Family Stories', *Washington Post*, July 29, 1990: 'If we want our children to grow up strong, secure, and upright...; if we want to show them paths out of moral chaos, we should scour our family histories and tell them stories of the heroes we find there.'
32. Ralph Abernathy, *And the Walls Came Tumbling Down*, New York: Harpur and Row, 1989. See illuminating review by R J Neuhaus, *Commentary* (NY), February 1990, pp 60ff, and discussion of Abernathy's significance by Philip Rieff, 'The Newer Noises of War in the Second Culture Camp', *Yale Journal of Law and the Humanities*. 1991, vol 3, pp 315-388.

33. Bell, op cit.
34. 'There is not an outward sign of politeness which has not a profound moral foundation', quoted in Lukacs, op cit, p 82.
35. Cf Richard Pipes, Baird Professor of History at Harvard: 'The "masses" everywhere readily take to American culture because its value-free, hedonistic ethic has the effect of emancipating the individual from the confines of family and community as well as the constraints of religion'. *Partisan Review*, New York, LXI, 1, 1994, p 168. See also Jonathan Solomon, 'Brave New Digital World', *The Tablet*, London, March 4, 1989, p 245; and Giovanni Sartori on Ortega y Gasset's *Revolt of the Masses* (1930): 'Ortega's philosophy was "aristocratic" in the Greek meaning of the term: it extolled excellence. But his distinction between leading minorities and masses cuts across social classes. Ortega's *aristoi* were conceived ascetically, as exemplary individuals defined by obligations, not by rights. Conversely, the mass man was assimilated by Ortega to the indulged heir of noble families. And despite much debunking, his portrait of a new man who for the first time in history takes everything for granted, who enjoys benefits without being solidary with the conditions that are conducive to such benefits, who refuses to grow up to his responsibilities, and who behaves as a spoiled child, as an ungrateful and undeserving heir, remains a powerful and highly insightful diagnosis'. *The Theory of Democracy Revisited*, Chatham NJ: Chatham House, 1987, p 27.
36. 'First and forgotten', conservatives have long been worried about the family. See, eg, *The Family: America's Hope*, with essays by diverse hands, including Michael Novak and James Hitchcock, Rockford, Illinois: The Rockford College Institute, 1979. On the possiblity of a traditionalist, especially Envangelical-Catholic, alliance, see Hunter, op cit, and 'Evangelicals and Catholics Together: A Declaration', *First Things*, New York, 43, May 1994, pp 15-22.

Chapter 11

1. As an example of how manners can be antimanners, the author of this chapter encountered after a lapse of years an old friend, a Jesuit priest. Moved with joy, he proceeded to kiss the Jesuit on both cheeks as one would a long-lost Orthodox brother. To the amusement of friends and bystanders, this greeting (perhaps because of recent scandals regarding certain acts of carnality on the part of Roman clerics) was received with some shock and disorientation.
2. Here the author reports the puzzlement of a secular friend who, without knowledge about the background of the behaviour, observed the author as an Indian nurse who looked not at all to be his kin, discovered he was Orthodox and responded with the exclamation, 'my brother!' which was followed by mutual heartfelt kisses on both cheeks and the author's exclamation 'my sister!' For one Calvinist observer, this act of courtesy between members of one spiritual family seemed out of place and unseemly.

3. Alasdair MacIntyre, *After Virtue*, Notre Dame, Ind: University of Notre Dame Press, 1981.
4. In this essay, I use the term post-modernity to underscore our failure to share, and our recognition that we no longer share, a universal moral narrative or common cultural perspective. Here I follow one suggestion of Lyotard: 'In contemporary society and culture — postindustrial society, postmodern culture — the question of the legitimation of knowledge is formulated in different terms. The grand narrative has lost its credibility, regardless of what mode of unification it uses, regardless of whether it is a speculative narrative or a narrative of emancipation.' Jean-François Lyotard, *The Postmodern Condition*, (trans G Bennington and B Massumi), Manchester: Manchester University Press, 1984, p 37.
5. This account of moral strangers, moral friends, and the character of moral discourse in a world fractured by diverse moral visions is developed at greater length in *The Foundations of Bioethics*, 2nd ed, New York: Oxford, 1996.
6. Ibid.
7. H T Engelhardt Jr and M A Rie, 'Selling Virtue: Ethics as a Profit Maximising Strategy in Health Care Delivery', *Journal of Health and Social Policy*, 4, 1992, pp 27-35.
8. See H T Engelhardt Jr, 'The Yuppie as a Prophet of a Secular Tradition for Health Care', in *Bioethics and Secular Humanism: The Search for a Common Morality*, London: SCM Press, 1991, pp 33-40.
9. Alasdair MacIntyre, *Whose Justice? Which Rationality?*, Notre Dame, Ind: University of Notre Dame Press, 1988, p 388.
10. Sidonius, *Poems and Letters*, Book II.ix, (trans W B Anderson), Cambridge, Mass: Harvard, 1980, vol 1, pp 451-457, 461.

The Social Affairs Unit is an independent research and educational trust committed to the promotion of lively and wide-ranging debate on social affairs. Its authors — over 200 — have analyzed the factors which make for a free and orderly society in which enterprise can flourish. Current areas of work include consumer affairs, the critical appraisal of welfare and public spending and problems of freedom and personal responsibility.

Gentility Recalled is the third title in its series on the problems of social order. The first, **The Loss of Virtue: moral confusion and social disorder in Britain and America** won first prize in the prestigious Sir Antony Fisher Awards for the best book from a think tank world-wide in 1994. The second, **This Will Hurt: the restoration of virtue and civic order** received widespread critical acclaim in Britain, Europe and North America.

'The Social Affairs Unit is famous for driving its coach and horses through the liberal consensus, scattering intellectual picket lines as it goes. It is equally famous for raising questions which strike most people most of the time as too dangerous or too difficult to think about'

The Times (London)

The Social Affairs Unit
Suite 5/6 1st Floor
Morley House
314-322 Regent Street
London W1R 5AB

The Acton Institute for the Study of Religion and Liberty, founded in April 1990, is named in honour of Sir John Emerich Edward Dalberg Acton, 1st Baron Acton of Aldenham (1834-1902), the historian of freedom. The mission of the Institute is to promote a society that embraces civil liberties and free market economics. To that end the Institute seeks to stimulate dialogue among religious, business and scholarly communities and to familiarize those communities, particularly students and seminarians, with the ethical foundations of political liberty and free market economics. It also serves as a clearing house of ideas for entrepreneurs interested in the ethical dimensions of their vital economic and commercial activities.

Lord Acton understood that liberty is 'the delicate fruit of a mature civilization' and that in every age the progress of religious, economic and political liberty is challenged, even threatened by its adversaries. Likewise, in our own age, liberty is under constant siege. It is our hope that by demonstrating the compatibility of religion, liberty, and free economic activity, religious leaders and entrepreneurs can forge an alliance that will serve to foster and secure an open, free and virtuous society.

The Acton Institute
The Waters Building
1612 Ottowa NW Suite 450K
Grand Rapids
Michigan 49503